108

The Learning of History

The Learning of History

D. G. Watts

Senior Counsellor,
The Open University

LONDON AND BOSTON
ROUTLEDGE & KEGAN PAUL

First published 1972
by Routledge & Kegan Paul Ltd
Broadway House, 68-74 Carter Lane
London EC4V 5EL and
9 Park Street,
Boston, Mass. 02108, U.S.A.
Printed in Great Britain by
Northumberland Press Ltd
Gateshead

ISBN 0 7100 7433 6
Lib. Card Cat. No. SBN 72 90118

Contents

CONTENTS

To the memory of E. G. Watts

1903-1971

1
Introduction

While I was writing this chapter, I noticed the front page of a cheap commercial comic devoted to an illustrated life of Charles I; on the same day, a colour magazine was running another of its series on the history of England. A news item told us that the B.B.C. was to spend £500,000 on the production of a television series about twentieth-century history. Another item reported that a recent survey of children's reading habits showed that the most popular book was *Black Beauty*, followed by *Little Women* and *Treasure Island*, with *Oliver Twist*, *Jane Eyre* and *Tom Sawyer* not far down the list, all of which are novels with historical themes or settings (*Guardian*, 31 July and 4 September 1971). And yet, at the same time, specialized journals on history teaching have echoed with phrases like 'malaise and discomfort' and 'doubt and discontent' (Barraclough, 1966, p. 6). History has long been a criticized and controversial academic subject, but it has never been more popular. This book sets out to explore, and in part to explain, this paradox; in particular, to try to resolve the dilemma it creates for teachers of history in schools (Fines, 1969, p. v). Of four main areas of debate—a debate among philosophers on the nature of the subject and its material, a debate among historians on the nature and methods of their craft, a debate among educationalists on whether and how to teach history to children, and a debate about whether and how a mass audience can properly be involved with history—this book will be primarily concerned with education, but will make extended references to the rest.

History had hardly emerged as an academic discipline in Britain when Jane Austen's Catherine Morland pointed to one aspect of the paradox: 'I often think it odd that it should be so dull, for a great deal of it must be invention' (*Northanger Abbey*). And her contemporary, Sir Walter Scott, in the process of becoming the most popular of writers of 'invented' history, was already well aware of the problems. He contrasted the desultory, indolent reading of his hero Edward Waverley, not only with the need for 'concentrating the powers of his mind for earnest investigation', but also with what was happening in the schools, where 'children are taught the driest doctrines by the insinuating method of instructive games ... the history of England is now reduced to a game at cards'. But the most interesting aspect of this passage is that in spite of his criticisms, Scott's sympathies, seemingly reflecting the autobiographical experience of the period when he read Percy's *Reliques* under the plane tree at Kelso, are with Waverley, with his 'brilliancy of fancy and vivacity of talent', whose 'powers of apprehension were so uncommonly quick as almost to resemble intuition' (*Waverley*, 1829). Scott was here touching on important features of the learning of history which will be discussed in Chapter 2.

Hugh Trevor-Roper, while speaking eloquently of the importance of Scott's better work, with its nice balance of imagination and realism, to the study of history, has reminded us of the travesty of history, the tushery, of his worst work (1971). But there is something to learn from the power even of bad history. Across the Atlantic, the results of Scott's own 'brilliancy of fancy' had, according to Mark Twain, a devastating effect on the character of half a nation. In his *Life on the Mississippi* (1874) Twain first tells us that *Ivanhoe* was among the books commonly found on Southern bookshelves. Then, after a few ranging shots at 'Walter Scott and his knights and beauty and chivalry and so on' and 'his medieval business', he launched this escalating assault (Ch. 46):

> Then comes Sir Walter Scott with his enchantments, and ... sets the world in love with dreams and phantoms ... with the sillinesses and emptinesses, sham grandeurs, sham gauds, and sham chivalries of a brainless and worthless long vanished society. He did measureless harm; more real and lasting harm, perhaps, than any other individual that ever wrote ... Sir Walter Scott had so large a hand in making Southern character, as it existed before the war, that he is great measure responsible for the war. It seems a little harsh toward a dead man to say that we never should have had any war but for Sir Walter; and yet something of a plausible argument might perhaps be made in support of that wild proposition ... A curious exemplification of the power of a single book for good or harm is shown in the effects wrought by Don Quixote and those wrought by Ivanhoe. The first swept the world's admiration for the medieval chivalry silliness out of existence; and the other restored it. As far as our South is concerned, the good work done by Cervantes is pretty nearly a dead letter, so effectually has Scott's pernicious work undermined it.

This, of course, is a splendid bit of fun, but characteristically Twain is at the same time making some serious and acute points. He is concerned with the power of writing on men's behaviour, in particular, with the effect of the vicarious experience offered by the historical novel, in which, for many people, medieval knights might act, in sociological terms, as a reference group, a guide to behaviour.

When Twain went on to parody the medieval romance in *A Yankee at King Arthur's Court*, his readers quickly forgot the parody, and just enjoyed the story. Twain also made pugnacious attacks on two of Scott's disciples, Captain Marryat and Fennimore Cooper, but their justly exposed 'literary offences' did not prevent them being enormously successful writers, nor, like Scott and Twain himself, from becoming posthumous story writers for popular television. In England, G. A. Henty was an even more widely read historical novelist than Marryat. Henty must be one of the very few non-classic writers of the 1890s still being reprinted in cheap editions in the 1970s. He played the part in Edwardian popular culture that Twain supposed Scott had played in Southern culture. And if we indulge in a similar flight of fancy, we can see the 'contemptible little army' of 1914 sustained in another hideous war by memories of the patriotic heroes of *The Young Franc-Tireurs* and *Jack Archer*.

One of Henty's readers who was mercifully not fit enough to go to France was C. S. Forester, as prolific a historical novelist in the twentieth century as Scott and Henty had been in the nineteenth, and another supplier of stories for film and radio. Forester illustrates part of our thesis, that there is a mass audience for imaginative work with a careful and detailed historical background. But also, like Scott, he gives us some suggestive clues to the process of historical learning. Forester describes how at the age of five he read 'the thrilling serials of S. Walkley, about pirates and Spaniards and shiploads of treasure ... [and] the French Revolution'. By the time he was seven he had 'formed the habit ... of reading one book a day at least ... The standard authors like Henty and Ballantyne and Collingwood ... and Robert Leighton ... were devoured in enormous gulps'. When he was eight, while playing wars with lead soldiers and paper ships, he wrote 'Army lists covering scores of pages of foolscap [and] Naval Operations orders ... in a style copied from the letters in Laughton's Letters of Lord Nelson' (1967, Ch. 2). Here then were the origins of a successful and influential historical novelist, and a modestly successful historian, who in slightly different personal circumstances might have become a professional historian.

But Forester also writes interestingly about the conception and gestation of his novels:

> There is a more thrilling mood when books are more usually conceived ... The pulse rate definitely increases, there is a sensation of warmth under the skin, there is a feeling of activity which makes it desirable to walk aimlessly about, there is a consciousness that the brain is working more rapidly ... And the moment when consciousness of this condition is realised, it is usually realised simultaneously that the germ of an idea is present ... If the mood is allowed to simmer down the germ remains, possibly—probably—forgotten for a moment. Then recurrently it bobs up again, and at every reappearance it is more developed, mainly without conscious effort on the part of the author. He picks it up and looks at it, so to speak, turns it over, and drops it back again, possibly after adding one or two slight improvements. Finally, the idea presents itself as fully formed as unconscious work will make it, sometimes quite complete, more usually needing just a little conscious effort on the author's part to finish it off. (ibid., Ch. 18)

Later in life, Forester was to use a maritime metaphor for such ideas:

> It sinks into the horrid depths of my subconscious like a waterlogged timber into the slime at the bottom of

a harbour, where it lies alongside others which have preceded it. Then, periodically—but by no means systematically—it is hauled up for examination along with its fellows, and sooner or later, some timber is found with barnacles growing on it. (ibid., p. 177)

Forester is interesting too on the role of visualization in his work:

What is it that forms those words? What is going on in my mind as I write them? I have no doubt that in my case it is a matter of a series of visualizations. Not two dimensional, as if looking at a television screen: three dimensional, perhaps, as if I were a thin, invisible ghost walking about a stage while a play is in actual performance. I can move where I like, observe the actors from the back as well as the front, from prompt side as well as opposite prompt, noting their poses and their concealed gestures and their speeches ... I can run through a scene again like a Hollywood director in his chair in a projection room, and when I have finished with a scene I discard it and conjure up another one, devised in my mind all those weeks ago in the happy period of construction. It is really reporting for all the invention has already been carried out ... (ibid., p. 182)

Forester was of course a highly professional writer, working to a daily quota of words, but like Scott and Anthony Trollope, he was able to draw in his professional activity on a vivid and fertile imagination.

One contemporary historian who is very concerned to advocate professional standards to his students is Arthur Marwick. But from time to time Marwick shows that his own thinking processes may not be so very different from Forester's. He quotes with approval Denys Hay: 'The hall-mark of the historically-minded person is an itch for the concrete, a desire to get behind generalizations to the facts upon which they are based and to establish an almost physical relationship with the texture of earlier times'. Marwick himself says that 'where we say that some article or person or event that you are describing is concrete, we mean that you have described it with such clarity that we can practically visualize, perhaps almost touch it, in our own minds', and he has a revealing little aside on the importance of colour in bringing history alive (Marwick *et al.*, 1971). We may guess that the psychological phenomena called eidetic imagery and synæthesia play an important part in the thinking of many historians. I shall be returning to these aspects of history in discussing imagery in Chapter 2 and stereotypes in Chapter 5.

In considering the place of history in popular culture we could go on beyond Hornblower, to discuss novels such as *Gone With the Wind*, the musical *Camelot*, television documentaries like *The First World War* and plays about Henry VIII, Elizabeth and Marlborough. And this huge audience is not just a passive one. The sales of paperbacks on Victoria and Mary Queen of Scots are the envy of most popular novelists. The interest in popular archaeology associated with the first series of 'Animal, Vegetable and Mineral' has recently entered a new phase. In the past ten years there has been a similar boom in industrial archaeology, and new museums of rural life and folk museums spring up even more quickly than wildlife parks. History continues to be the most popular of evening class subjects, and at the same time thousands of enthusiastic history students rush lemming-like towards a problematic employment market. If Mark Twain had lived, he might have supposed that Walter Scott was responsible for more than a civil war.

Criticisms

And yet the anxieties remain. *History in Danger, History Betrayed?*, *A Crisis in the Humanities* run the book titles (which have of course much smaller sales than John Prebble's *Culloden*). What is supposed to be wrong? (Price, 1968; Booth, 1969; Plumb, 1964).

We can begin by admitting that some of us have deserved the witticisms we have had to endure from generations of schoolboy heroes (Price, 1968, p. 344):

> Bunter! ... What king succeeded Edward the Fourth on the throne of England?
> Bunter cudgelled his fat brains ...
> Answer me Bunter.
> George the Fifth, sir, answered Bunter, taking a shot at a venture.
> What?
> I—I mean ... Bunter read in his form master's expressive countenance that his shot had missed the mark. I—I mean—I didn't mean George the Fifth, sir—I—I meant Charles the Third.
> Charles the Third! repeated Mr. Quelch, dazedly.
> Nunno! Again Bunter discerned that he had missed his mark. I—I meant to say Alfred, sir—King Alfred, who let the cakes burn! He—he said Kiss me Hardy!—and—and—never smiled again. (*Billy Bunter's Benefit*)

The splendid mockery in *1066 and All That* of history text-books, history teaching and history examinations succeeds so well because it comes uncomfortably close to the truth. How often is the criticism justified by the annual repetition of blackboard or dictated notes, copied into exercise books and regurgitated in exams: inadequate teaching, for unnecessary examinations, from bad text-books. 'Get out your grubby green books on *Europe 1815–1914*. Turn to page 157. Read section 93 on the Franco-Prussian War. Look carefully at the smudged grey portraits of Napoleon III and Bismarck. There will be a test at the end of the lesson.'

Here are two excerpts from students' essays about their

experience of learning history, not in the time of Scott and Jane Austen, but in the 1960s. Student A wrote:

Junior School history was thoroughly enjoyed by me because when we studied a certain topic, we were allowed a few lessons to develop what we had been told and so by the end of it we knew and really understood what we were being taught. What a change was felt when we moved to a grammar school! Here we went into a classroom at the beginning of a lesson, opened notebooks and were dictated notes from then to the end, often finishing off in the middle of a sentence only to carry on from there the next lesson. We were given no opportunity to ask questions and we often did not understand what had been told us.

Student B wrote:

At the [junior] school I attended, we were given a particular chapter to read and then we had to write up short notes on the context. What the teacher really wanted was a simple date and the event opposite. But there were many in the class, myself included, who found the chapter on Clive of India and Black Hole of Calcutta stimulating enough to write almost the whole chapter again in our own words, including how elephants were used as battering rams ... However in our eagerness to re-create these scenes again in our note-books, more pages were used up than the teacher wished, and further history notes were strictly limited to the stark date and event. As a result, many of us began to lose interest in these lessons.

Second, history teachers have allowed themselves to be rattled by professional historians. Many teachers are historians manqués, and they take rather seriously the things that professionals say. But of course professional historians are writing primarily for other professional historians, and so far as they discuss teaching, they are discussing the training of apprentice professional historians (Elton, 1967, p. 182). They know very little and think rather less about the teaching of the subject to the ordinary child. Looked at from the point of view of popular history, a professional historian's writing about history, for instance Elton's *The Practice of History*, though sharp and pertinent in its own field, seems strangely irrelevant to what is going on. Professional historians, like scholars in many other fields, have tried to enhance their subject's academic status by denying its popular character and erecting barriers of professional language and technique between themselves and the mass audience. In some subjects, in philosophy perhaps, in behaviourist psychology, possibly now in the new geography, the professionals may have succeeded in putting the barriers up. But history, in spite of the efforts of professionals, has not been cut off from the popular roots from which it draws its vitality. To change the metaphor, narrow theories of history tend to saw off the branch that we are all sitting on. What is required is a definition of the subject which convincingly encompasses 'soft' popular history at one end, and 'hard' professional history at the other; and this is the purpose of Chapter 3.

This attitude among professional historians has a number of origins. There is the continuous escalation of 'standards' within the academic community. An Oxbridge M.A. or a first class degree are no longer an adequate qualification for full professional status, nor even is a single higher degree (see the *Guardian*, 13 August 1971). A second higher degree, some technical qualification in economics or statistics, research experience in an overseas university, a list of publications 'as long as your arm', these are now the entry requirements for the academic race. From such a position it is almost impossible to see the other end of the historical spectrum: indeed it is actually dangerous to recognize that it exists. A single injudicious article about children and you may be damned as 'unsound', with the prospect of a Senior Lectureship receding for ever; far safer to be heard using the words 'scholarly' and 'rigorous' at suitable opportunities. The opening of new universities has actually reinforced this process of professionalization, for history departments in new universities could not risk being compared unfavourably with the older universities or with one another. At the same time, the sense of competition for esteem with the sciences, with economics, even with sociology, has sharpened the desire to represent history as a highly disciplined corpus of knowledge. And this defensiveness has been accentuated by the same factors that have been bringing pressure on school history—an uneasy feeling that too much history teaching is bad, an uncertainty about the theoretical status of the subject and about the influence of public policy. Cautious discussion of reform normally revolves around the reshuffling of a familiar pack of periods, topics and special subjects. Professional history, in fact, is in danger of getting itself into an impasse, and discussion of ways out of the impasse is not helped by the contemptuous attitude of many professional historians towards educational theory.

A third source of the pressure on history teaching is public policy. This can be seen both in the promotion of other subjects within schools and colleges, and in measures directed against history itself. The policy's rationale is found in the supposed shortage of mathematicians, scientists and technicians, and of teachers of those subjects, and its influence can be seen in the anxious scrutiny of the figures which from time to time show swings among schoolchildren and students towards or away from science courses. The policy operates at many levels: by making history an optional rather than a required subject in examinations; by different gradings for heads of history departments and for heads of science and mathematics;

by discontinuing history courses in some colleges of education; by recognizing other subjects (but not history) for degree-level courses; by opening new institutions without history departments, and by making grants for research in subjects other than history. In a more positive way, there is genuine concern about the job prospects of both schoolchildren and those undergraduates who have been seduced by this attractive subject, a conviction that it is very much in young people's interests if, instead, the girls can be persuaded to do a secretarial course, the boys an engineering course, or the undergraduates a supplementary diploma in social welfare.

The fourth source of pressure on traditional history is the advocacy of alternative syllabuses. Such a new syllabus may be one of sufficient novelty, made up perhaps of topics from contemporary, international or Afro-Asian history, that it involves the abandonment of the bulk of recognized historial material. Geoffrey Barraclough's well-known remark about 'mulling over Simon de Montfort for ever' was made in the context of his advocacy of world history (1966, p. 7; 1967). More far reaching are the various arguments for projects, topics and integrated days in the lower school, and for integrated courses in social studies, environmental studies, liberal studies and the like for older children. Again, these developments have both negative and positive features. They provide, on the one hand, over-convenient solutions for the problem of what to do with currently embarrassing subjects like history and religious studies. On the other hand, they offer sound reasons why integrated work should have a place on school timetables, and the periods presently devoted to history may seem relatively poorly defended positions into which the new work can be fitted (Watts, 1969). It is, of course, a weakness as well as a strength of history that it can be regarded as part of almost every other subject. The view taken in this volume is that both history and integrated studies deserve a place in a school curriculum, and with flexible planning there is no reason why they should not coexist there.

The fifth area of criticism, and the one which has probably been most corrosive of school history teaching in recent years, is that associated with certain views about learning and child development. It is said, for instance, that history is nearly all about adults and their behaviour; schoolchildren do not know what it is like to be an adult, and do not understand adults' behaviour, so they cannot understand history (Elton, 1967, p. 182). Small children, again, cannot distinguish historical stories from fairy stories, and if the history we teach is to be confused with fairy stories this will instil in the children the wrong attitudes to the subject. It is said, too, that small children cannot reason systematically—but history is a subject which makes much use of systematic reasoning—so it is impossible to teach it properly. It is suggested that children learn from immediately observable objects rather than from words or ideas; and as history is essentially non-observable, they cannot learn it. Again, it is supposed that small children do not understand chronology or the concept of time—but history depends on considerations of time—and so children cannot understand it. Finally, it is said, history is about people who are dead, and about the processes of death and dying, the deaths for instance of Boudicca and Bede and Nelson; but children may not have a proper concept of death until the age of nine or ten, so that they cannot really follow what is happening (Anthony, 1940, p. 84).

Propositions like these are subject to more detailed analysis in Chapter 2. I want to make only some general points now. First, arguments of this kind seem to assume that adults *know*, while children are *ignorant*. But what *do* adults know about other human beings, about the passage of time, or about death? The position is in fact that children know a little about these concepts, and adults know a little more. If we taught history to people with a refined understanding of adult behaviour and the passage of time, we should probably only teach it as part of preparation-for-retirement courses; we should certainly not teach it to undergraduates. Second, arguments like these beg the question whether, if children are ignorant of something, it is not our business to help them to learn it. And if we say that we do not know how to teach such very difficult concepts, we should not suppose that it is impossible; it may only be that in these fields our theory, research and curriculum development are still as inadequate as the children's understanding. If we ask how children *do* come to acquire what they ultimately know about adult behaviour, time, death and the like, the answer clearly is that they are learning all the time. Some of this learning is informal, in listening to parents and neighbours and by sharing experiences with them. But some of it is formal, and is acquired by taking part in lessons, listening to the teacher and reading the books the teacher recommends. It would be a shocking failure of responsibility if the teaching profession said it could do nothing in these most difficult learning areas.

Within the teaching experience then, children come to learn more about the behaviour of adults, the passage of time, and death—by listening to stories, doing a little geography, some drama and verse, discussing religion and especially I think, by doing history. The school introduces us to children of many lands, and to those old faithfuls of the social studies periods, the postman, the milkman and the policeman. We grow up, too, by meeting the Wife of Bath, and King Lear, and Becky Sharp. But I would contend that we grow up most of all by marching with Harold from victory at Stamford Bridge to defeat at Hastings, by following Joan from Orleans to the stake, by sympathizing with Elizabeth in her marriage dilemma and with Cromwell's reluctance to take the throne, and by getting just a sense of what it meant to be Gladstone, 'an old man in a hurry'. These points will be pursued in Chapter 4.

Here then is the paradox. History is a subject which is perhaps, after sport, the most important ingredient of international mass communications; which is capable not only of exciting millions of people by its colour, romance, drama and narrative power, but also of stimulating lively interest in more extended documentary treatment. And yet (it would be unbelievable if we did not read it almost daily) many of its practitioners cannot find a theory which encompasses this interest, are of a mind to confine the subject to a learned minority, are not sure which bits of it can safely be taught to young children, or indeed whether young people are intellectually capable of appreciating it at all. The following chapters offer suggestions for the resolution of these issues.

(Extracts from *Long Before Forty* by C. S. Forester, are reprinted by permission of A. D. Peters and Company.)

2

Thinking and the learning of history

Probably the most damaging of the contemporary attacks on school history is that arising from certain propositions about child psychology and development. In order to answer these criticisms, it will be necessary in this chapter first to establish a view of the nature of thinking and intelligence, and then to show the relevance of this view to school history teaching.

Empiricist-progressivism

The propositions of what we shall call empiricist-progressivism may be summarized in this way: the infant has innate drives similar to those of animals towards the understanding of his surroundings. Being animal, these drives are effective in the physical world, but are not, in infancy, of an intellectual kind. They cannot be manipulated consciously by either the learner or a teacher, so that the child 'matures' or 'develops' rather than 'learns'. The drives operate by the construction of increasingly complex cognitive structures about the nature of the physical environment, the child building a picture of reality out of physical (sensori-motor) experience, acquired during its own activity. These structures are in early childhood crude, 'egocentric', 'autistic', and are quite inadequate for understanding concepts outside the immediate environment. In due course the cognitive structures become self-sustaining, that is, take on the character of abstract thought, but this process is only completed in adolescence. Not until then can the child effectively deal with material unrelated to its own concrete experience. Small children therefore do not possess the intellectual or cognitive equipment by which history can be assimilated. This point of view can be illustrated from a well-known textbook:

It follows ... from the insistence that thought is internalized action, that experience, activity, construction, assembly and sorting out of material objects and visible entities are a necessary precursor of thought. This brings us again to the function of primary school education in developing the thinking powers of children. The artificial nature of language and number has been mentioned. It is all the more important therefore that activity and construction form the basis of primary education, not only to close the gap between actual thinking levels and the stereotyped use of language and number, but also to provide a naturally developed, surely based foundation for the more abstract formal thinking of adolescence. The primary school child has to reach fully the state of equilibrium of concrete thought before he is ready and equipped to adolescent and adult thought ... (and in applying the argument) ... history ... could form a rewarding subject to junior school pupils, provided the emphasis were on classifying and finding differences between the observable data. (Peel, 1960, pp. 86-7; see also Hallam, 1967, p. 183; Peel, 1967)

Piaget and the Piagetians

Peel, like other writers in this vein, leans heavily on the work of Piaget. Indeed, discussions of this subject echo with the phrase 'Piaget says that . . .' This is not the place to attempt a general evaluation of Piaget's work or its relevance to pedagogy, but some general points can be made.

Piaget, as will be seen, has himself been aware of various alternative approaches to the evolution of thinking, but has found it necessary to limit his researches to only some of them. His work, though interesting and important, is not the only reputable approach to the problems of thinking and learning. To take only three examples, neither Ryle's *The Concept of Mind*, Hebb's *The Organization of Behaviour*, nor Price's *Thinking and Experience*, all modern classics in their fields, contain a single reference to Piaget. It is possible for the history teacher to construct an alternative model of thinking and learning about his subject, in which Piaget's work is only part of the evidence, but which is nevertheless based on serious work and sound sources.

It is noteworthy that Piaget has shown little interest in drawing pedagogic conclusions from his own work. There is therefore no authoritative source for what these should be, and those conclusions which have been drawn reflect the preconceptions of the interpreters. In particular, Piaget's work has been commonly interpreted in the empiricist-progressive tradition, which existed long before him (Sullivan, 1967, pp. 32, 34). We can retrace this tradition to Locke's empiricism and see that it has for centuries been a 'progressive' premise that learning takes place by the gradual accumulation of sense impressions, by the child's active exploration of his environment, his manipulation of concrete objects and his 'discovery' of relationships between them (Watts, 1969, Ch. 2). From Locke to Whitehead and since, verbal learning and book learning, necessarily important in history teaching, have been suspected and criticized: 'I hate books', wrote Rousseau; 'they only teach us about things we know nothing about.'

This empiricist element in progressivism has been re-inforced by a naturalist or romantic strand, which has directed attention to the propriety of learning from nature; even Wordsworth, who greatly valued books in his own education, urged his rationalist acquaintance, 'Up! up! my friend, and quit your books.' In the late nineteenth and early twentieth centuries, these views were again rein-forced by an experimental tradition, which has attempted to draw conclusions about effective human learning from tests on rats and monkeys, who manifestly do not read books, and from experiments with human beings in essen-tially physical situations. Dewey's definition of thinking as 'problem-solving' gave this empiricist system a theore-tical rationale. In the mid-twentieth century, Piaget's work was absorbed by this tradition, though in fact, as Nathan Isaacs saw, his evidence might have implications which run counter to it (1961, p. 33). If Piaget shows us, for instance, that the child cannot learn history until he has mastered certain concepts, the progressives conclude that we must delay teaching the subject until he has them. But it can be argued that what Piaget has done is to pin-point those concepts we should seek to develop in the child in order to *accelerate* his learning.

A more general criticism of Piaget is that he has made an over-logical, over-rational definition of thinking, and has thereafter neglected those cognitive processes which fall outside his definition:

> Piaget's restriction of 'conceptual thought' to what Price regards as full-dress, symbolic, logical thinking seems less happy ... the possibility of there being at least two types of thought process ... remains a burning question at the core not only of experimental and genetic psy-chology but of current speculation in many fields. (Reeves, 1965, pp. 295, 36)

It can then be pointed out that the neglected cognitive processes seem to be precisely those which might give an adequate account of the learning of history, literature and related subjects (Boyle, 1969, p. 145). What follows is an attempt to suggest a model within which such cognitive processes can take their place.

Association

For our alternative to the empiricist-progressive model we shall make use of a concept as old as empiricism itself, that of association. The term has been used in many ways in the history of psychology; the usage here is not that of 'classical associationism' but rather that of 'the association of ideas'. Association will be considered as an element in imagination, intuition and creativity. The propositions put forward are that many, if not most, cognitive processes in both children and adults are of the nature of spontaneous associations of images and concepts; that not only can people think associatively, but that much day-to-day thinking is of such a kind : that we use rational or logical thinking much less often than the problem-solving model would imply, and that 'intelligent' thinking is the result of the fusion of rational *and* associative elements, what Galton called 'fluency'.

Our difficulties in recognizing and giving a place to associative thinking arise partly from the inadequate paradigms into which such processes have to be fitted. One such scheme, a developmental one, looks like this :

Intelligence (effective abstract thinking)
↑
Formal thinking (abstract thinking)
↑
Concrete thinking (rational thinking about objects) to age 11-12
↑
'Intuitive' thinking (e.g. association) to age 7-8
↑
Sensori-motor thinking (by manipulation and activity)

In this model, 'intuitive' thinking is something crude which has to be given up during development. Another diagram, this time for the adult mind, looks like this:

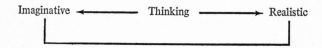

Imaginative ←——————— Thinking ————————→ Realistic

The trouble with this model, a characteristic empiricist-progressive one, is that it makes it difficult to be both imaginative and realistic, and seems to imply that one has to be either an artist or a scientist. An alternative model of adult thinking, combining elements of the other two, might look like this:

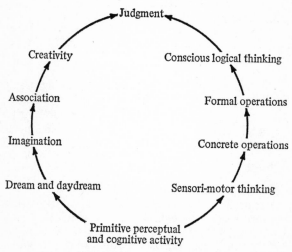

Judgment

Creativity — Conscious logical thinking

Association — Formal operations

Imagination — Concrete operations

Dream and daydream — Sensori-motor thinking

Primitive perceptual and cognitive activity

This diagram both recognizes the long-standing distinction between 'synthetic' and 'analytic' thinking, between *interpretateurs* and *simplistes* (Wiseman, 1967, p. 198), and suggests their fruitful interaction. For brevity, we shall

21

adopt McKellar's terminology of A and R-thinking for the two modes, while defining them not in the tendentious form of 'autistic thinking v. reality thinking' but in the more objective form 'associative v. rational' (1957, 1968).

Interest in associative thinking has a long and highly respectable history. Binet, William James, Spearman, Thurstone and Burt are among the distinguished names on a line which begins with Galton's *Inquiries into Human Faculty* (see Reeves, 1965, Ch. 6). Binet thought that:

> Modifications are continually taking place within us, which transmit unconscious impressions to our brain. And these diverse impressions are capable of suggesting ideas which appear all of a sudden in the light of consciousness, without our being able to guess at their origin. Perhaps our ideas most frequently originate thus, for they seem to summarize a work that goes on in the night of the unconscious. (quoted in Reeves, 1965, p. 198)

Reeves makes the point that to Binet 'thinking appeared ... in some degree the activity of the whole personality in which action, feeling and unconscious mental attitudes play a vital (though not exclusive) role' (ibid., p. 198). Binet's American contemporary William James wrote (1904, p. 351):

> It is by no means easy to decide just what is meant by reason, or how the peculiar process called reasoning differs from other thought sequences which may lead to similar results. Much of our thinking consists of trains of images suggested one by another, of a sort of spontaneous revery ... This sort of thinking leads nevertheless to rational conclusions both practical and theoretical.

But in spite of its respectable beginning, work on this theme has been markedly neglected. Burt has discussed this neglect. About productive association he writes: 'here is ... another field of cognitive activity calling for far closer analytic study than it has hitherto received', and on reproductive imagination: 'strange to say, comparatively few factorial studies have been made by later investigators' (Wiseman, 1967, p. 202). McKellar (1957, pp. 126, 183) finds the same phenomenon in his own field; he refers to 'Silberer's neglected but important studies', and to Holt's work, which 'has received too little attention from contemporary theorists'.

One reason for the neglect has been that the work of Freud, stemming in part from this very tradition, appeared to suggest that the importance of the associative processes lay in the affective rather than the cognitive field. This Freudian influence can be seen in an interesting analysis which Piaget made in 1926: 'Psycho-analysts have been led to distinguish two fundamentally different modes of thinking: *directed* or *intelligent thought*, and *undirected* or, as Bleuler proposes to call it, *autistic* thought'. Piaget noted a cognitive function of autism: 'there is interaction between these two modes of thought. Autism undoubtedly calls into being and enriches many inventions which are subsequently clarified and demonstrated by intelligence' (1926, pp. 43-7). Elsewhere he says: 'Logical activity isn't all there is to intelligence' (1928, pp. 201-2). But Piaget's own interests were to move towards directed thought, and he had, apparently unwittingly, adopted from his psycho-analytic background the tendentious terms 'autism' and 'egocentric', which have so misled some of his readers.

For thirty years, work on association and imagery was, as Burt noted, relatively neglected, the field being dominated by the empiricist-progressives, the behaviourists and the Piagetians. However, there was a lively renewal of

23

interest in this topic in the United States during the 1950s under the leadership of Guilford, the field being commonly called 'creativity'. This interest was associated with criticism of the earlier notion that there was one form of intelligence which could be measured as I.Q., and with the suggestion that there were several, perhaps many, different intellectual abilities or ways of thinking, each consisting of a battery of skills relevant to success in a particular kind of task. In practice, much of the recent work has tended to polarize the cognitive abilities in the earlier synthetic/ analytic manner, with terminology such as intuitive/ analytic, high creative/high I.Q., and divergent/convergent (Hudson, 1966). In Britain, this work has so far had only an indirect influence on pedagogy, largely because, in the empiricist-progressive tradition, creativity has continued to be associated with affective development, and thus with creative writing, modern drama, action painting and the like. In the field of cognitive skills, pedagogic theory is still dominated by activity and discovery with the aid of concrete objects.

Vygotsky

In the Soviet Union, however relatively detached from Western intellectual fashion, the psychologist Vygotsky was able to develop a more searching analysis of empiricist-progressivism. At the beginning of his *Thought and Language* he makes a point reminiscent of Binet about the relationship of intellect and affect:

> Their separation as subjects of study as a major weakness of traditional psychology since it makes thought processes appear as an autonomous flow of 'thoughts thinking themselves', segregated from the fullness of life, from the personal needs and interests, the inclinations and impulses, of the thinker ... [thus] the door is

closed on the issue of the causation and origin of our thoughts. (1962, p. 8)

This position enables Vygotsky to give much greater emphasis to the function of the pre-operational stage of childhood (to age 7-8) in the development of cognitive activity, showing, for instance, that autistic thought and egocentric speech are not primitive activities which must be discarded, but secondary developments with specific cognitive functions (ibid., pp. 18, 22, 45).

Vygotsky saw that irrational or illogical concepts were a necessary part of the child's intellectual growth, and gave a more positive role to the school and to verbal instruction in utilizing such concepts. He studied what he called the associative complex and the syncretic image, and the child's use of words to express them (ibid., p. 70). He points out their function: 'the syncretic schemata themselves, despite the fluctuations, lead the child gradually towards adaptation; their usefulness must not be underrated'. In his terminology, a pseudo-concept is 'a complex already carrying the germinating seed of a concept ... complex thinking begins the unification of scattered impressions; by organizing discrete elements of experience into groups, it creates a basis for later generalization' (ibid., pp. 23, 70, 76).

In the development of genuine concepts 'the decisive role is played by the word, deliberately used to direct all the part processes of advanced concept formation' (ibid., p. 78). This importance of language is one of the factors which give teaching a more active part in cognitive development than it has in the empiricist-progressive tradition: 'instruction is one of the principal sources of the school-child's concepts', and this involves teaching him 'many things that he cannot directly see or experience' (ibid., pp. 85-6). The non-spontaneous 'scientific' concepts taught in the school interact with the spontaneous concepts of the child in the process of mental development: 'it is our contention that the rudiments of systematization first enter the child's mind by way of his contact with scientific concepts and are then transferred to everyday concepts'. As for *readiness*, 'the only good kind of instruction is that which marches ahead of development and leads it; it must be aimed not so much at the ripe as at the ripening functions'. Language is indispensable to this instruction: 'thought is not merely expressed in words; it comes into existence through them' (ibid., pp. 93, 104, 125). This proposition in itself would direct our attention away from a preoccupation with concrete objects and activity, and towards pedagogic methods and subjects which employ language.

Vygotsky's analysis, then, suggests that there can be much useful instruction in the infant and lower junior school; that such instruction can and should employ the developing cognitive structures of children of that age; that verbal instruction is not only possible but necessary, and that many of the concepts developed will be of an abstract or non-environmental character.

Association and the child

We have seen that one of the problems of the Piagetian approach has been that it has regarded 'autistic' or 'intuitive' thinking as a primitive stage to be grown out of and treated as immature if revealed in adult life. We can now make some comments on this point:

1. A-thinking is not primitive, but a secondary stage, one of secondary perception (McKellar, 1957) or second-order learning (Watts, 1969). It is a remarkable achievement which enables the child to think abstractly through images, or in Bruner's terminology, icons. This is consonant with Vygotsky's interpretation of the role of autistic thinking and egocentric speech.

2. Koehler and Vygotsky have commented on the apparent paucity of images in the thinking of apes (Vygotsky, 1962, pp. 33, 36). As Thomson pointed out, 'perhaps the chief importance of imagery in human thinking is that ... of raising behaviour in the face of a problem above the level of animal trial-and-error' (1924, p. 90). It is precisely when the human infant begins to show signs of imaginative activity in dreams and play that in matched pairs he draws ahead of the young ape. Sensorimotor exploration has taken the child and the ape thus far together. But beyond this point it is not enough, and well before the appearance of operational thinking, imagery provides the child with cues to further development.

3. The intuitive stage is not therefore a static phase of irrational behaviour: it is the *necessary* stage of preparation for operational thinking. Associational thinking provides the pseudo-concepts from which genuine concepts are developed. It is out of a fusion of sensori-motor exploration with associational thinking that operational thinking emerges. So that if, in the school, we want to accelerate this development, we must enrich association as well as experience.

4. R-thinking does not extinguish A-thinking at age 7-8. To quote Vygotsky, 'even the normal adult, capable of using and forming concepts, does not consistently operate with concepts in his thinking ... the adult constantly shifts from conceptual to concrete, complex-like thinking. The transitional, pseudo-concept form of thinking is not confined to child thinking; we too resort to it very often in our daily life ... our daily speech continuously fluctuates between the ideals of mathematical and of imaginative harmony' (ibid., pp. 75, 127-8). R-thinking replaces A-thinking for some cognitive functions, fuses with it in others, but supplements it and remains the junior partner elsewhere.

5. In the empiricist scheme, R-thinking is thought of as increasing in power, the R^1 of sensori-motor learning developing into the R^4 of the intelligent adult. But it seems reasonable to suppose that A-thinking develops too, from the A^1 noises of the baby to the A^4 of Kubla Khan, or the manipulation of the teddy bear into the making of sculpture. Between the two modes there is an AR area of fusion, developing from the child's AR^1 deduction that the missing doll is in the toy box, to the AR^4 used in that combination of knowledge, experience and hunches which we call judgment in adult life. We may guess that these are the varied cognitive skills illustrated by Hudson's evidence, which distinguishes categories of intelligent convergers, of intelligent divergers, and of intelligent boys who were not discernibly one or the other (Hudson, 1966).

Association and the curriculum

It has long been clear that, as well as the operational, the child's mind has another dimension which in the past has been called fantasy or imagination. The cognitive functions of the imagination, however, have been underestimated or neglected by the theorists of the empiricist-progressive tradition. These writers have discussed fantasy in three ways. First, it can be regarded, as we have seen, as a crude, pre-rational phase, superseded by the development of operational thinking. It can also be seen as crucial to the proper development of the child's affective or emotional life—but not of his intellect. Or it can be viewed, in the Wordsworthian tradition, as essential to the growth of the child's aesthetic sensibilities—but again, not of his intellect. This has been one aspect of the romantic tendency to see a wall between intellect and culture, with on one side much talk of scientific objectivity, and on the other a wish 'to sow the seeds of ideas which could revolutionise a system coldly obsessed with facts' (see Watts, 1969, p. 47).

These attitudes have been reflected in the progressive curriculum. Topics dealing with the child's direct experience and with the evolution of operational thinking—discovery methods, experimental science, mathematics, environmental studies—are included; so are topics contributing to the child's expressive development—stories, poetry, drama, dance and art. History, apparently unrelated to the child's direct experience, and yet a rational or logical subject, is not (and to some extent geography, religion and aspects of literature have been in a similar position).

Various attempts have been made to remodel the teaching of history in this empiricist-progressive mould. History's expressive aspects have been brought out by the use of drama and mime; its concrete aspects in one way by art and model-making, in another way by environmental studies; and the place of history in the present life of the child has been explored through the teaching of contemporary history, international history and social studies. Now, most working historians have found these experiments inadequate as an approach to their subject, but have been hard put to it to explain why. The answer given here is that the experiments have been based on a faulty psychological model, one which works well for curriculum reform in mathematics and the physical sciences, but does not work for history and other humane disciplines. If, as has been argued, there is more than one kind of thinking, then perhaps the process of active discovery among concrete objects is only one way of developing cognitive skills, and the school curriculum should be less exclusively organized around that process than it has been in recent years.

Concept formation

Associational concepts can be described as formed from undirected perceptions, subconsciously stored, associatively sorted, precipitated into consciousness by language and often linked to the child's affective drives. There is constant interaction between these elements, and fantasy or imagination is one result of this interaction. Looking briefly at the affective component, two sets of drives may be postulated in the child:

1. Innate drives of an animal origin, leading the child to orientate himself to stimuli, to explore his environment, to satisfy his curiosity, and so on.

2. Subconscious drives of social or cultural origin, leading the child to want to show off, to please, to succeed, to do better than rivals, to create, to speculate in ambitious ways, and the like.

Even before he can use language, the child seems, in his play with dolls and other toys, to have developed a capacity to interpret his subconscious fantasies in terms of visual images, and so to use such images as symbols, or, to follow Bruner, as icons. The process is greatly accelerated with the acquisition of language: 'the child feels the need for words and, through his questions, actively tries to learn the signs attached to objects. He seems to have discovered the symbolic function of words' (Vygotsky, 1962, p. 43). He rapidly develops a three-way matching system, fantasy-icon-word, word-icon-fantasy, etc. This system enables the child, among other things, to make some sense of words in terms of fantasy and percepts, and to make some sense of perceptual experience in terms of fantasy and words.

'A child is able to grasp a problem, and to visualise the goal it sets, at an early stage in his development ... but the forms of thought that he uses in dealing with these tasks differ profoundly from the adult's' (ibid., p. 55). Pre-operational, associational thinking enables the child to make sense of non-observable, non-experienced, even of abstract concepts. Take, for instance, the concept snake. Very few infants have seen a snake; many will not even have seen a good photograph or an accurate drawing of a snake, and yet all will have the rough-and-ready snake concept. The acquisition of this concept exemplifies the process analysed above. There is clearly an emotional drive which leads the child towards conceptualization; there is a manifest symbolic or iconic content in the concept, and the word-symbol is then readily matched to the icon, and 'understood'. The same process in the field of natural history can be seen for instance in the concepts 'fox', 'wolf' and 'whale'; in geography, in 'forest', 'mountain', 'ocean' and 'Antarctica'; in religion, in 'death', 'heaven', 'Jesus' and 'God'; and in history, in 'the Stone Age', 'the Romans', 'knights' and 'Nelson'. In discussing their function in the curriculum, it is useful to call such concepts 'stereotypes'. Stereotypes are enriched by further associations, and refined and actualized by experience. In Vygotsky's words, 'these concepts are schematic and lack the rich content derived from personal experience. They are filled gradually, in the course of further schoolwork and reading' (ibid., p. 108).

We have suggested that in areas where direct experience and the manipulation of concrete objects are normal, areas in fact related to elementary mathematics, science and technology, the R-thinking analysis is persuasive and valuable. On the other hand, there are large areas of cognitive functioning where R-thinking does not, perhaps cannot,

THINKING AND THE LEARNING OF HISTORY

replace A-thinking, those for instance concerned with human relations, human society and speculative reasoning.

Much research has been done on the way the child develops its R-thinking abilities. On A-thinking, a good deal of work has been done with adults (McKellar, 1957, 1968), but very little on the conditions for its development in children. We must suppose that the child exercises its A-thinking with play, toys and the bedtime story (age 2-4). He goes on, in modern British conditions, to picture-books, comics and children's television (4-6). He develops and employs a vigorous sense of humour (6-7). Then he begins silent reading, and in the right kind of home or school, is launched into the imaginative world of the traditional British primers of A-thinking—Beatrix Potter, A. A. Milne, Kenneth Grahame, Lewis Carroll, C. S. Lewis and the like (8 onwards). From this point, A-thinking develops more specialized forms, the AA thinking of art, drama, poetry and creative writing, and the AR thinking of narrative literature, history, elementary science and current affairs. By age 11-12, children have powerful daydreams and strong combatative opinions in this AR field, which lead them into elaborate personal exploration of topics like archæ-ology, space-travel or the novels of Conan Doyle. It is in this sphere and at this age, rather than in R-thinking, that the advantaged child most obviously out-distances his dis-advantaged peer; from this point the university scholar-ships begin to be won and the seminal books written. And here we can link our argument about associational think-ing with Hudson's evidence of the historical ability of his divergent thinkers (1966).

Thinking and learning history

Let us now turn from the general discussion of thinking and learning to the connection between theories or learn-ing and the teaching of history.

32

1. The behaviourist or learning theory model, which provides useful clues to the teaching of accepted facts and established concepts, is of little help to the historian, most of whose 'facts' are uncertain and concepts debatable. Objective tests, programmed learning and teaching machines, in spite of the efforts to build 'debate' into them, are not likely to do more than occasionally supplement normal history teaching. Gagné's admirable book (1965), for instance, which might form a primer for teachers of science and languages, says little of value to the history teacher.

2. Dewey's problem-solving model is also inadequate. Much historical thinking is better described as a form of speculation, directed imagination or vicarious living. In any case, just because the material of history is uncertain and debatable, it is difficult, if not literally impossible, to solve problems in history. The historian can solve problems subsidiary to his subject, such as the date of a document, and he characteristically constructs a series of models for problem-solution. But history is much more concerned with problem-raising than problem-solving (see Chapter 3). History is a series of exercises in problem-raising and problem-solving rather than a problem-solving activity itself.

3. An expressive or affective approach is important in some aspects of history (see Chapter 4), but it cannot be the whole or the central aspect of the subject. Historians are at least some of the time concerned with the 'analysis', 'synthesis' and 'evaluation' of Bloom's cognitive domain; and drama or model-making can only contribute marginally to these processes.

4. The inadequacy of the empiricist-progressive model, with its use of activity, discovery and concrete objects, has already been indicated. Much interesting historical material is concrete and can be actively examined. But essentially, from the child's first encounter with 'Stig of the Dump' to

a mature historical work on medieval prisons, history is a subject 'in the head', one in which the past is reconstructed in second-order images and in which words are used to analyse and interpret the images.

A-thinking and history

The A-thinking model of history as a rich store of associative imagery enriched by reading and experience, later controlled and interpreted but not displaced by R-thinking, seems a more satisfactory basis for historical pedagogy than those already discussed. With its aid, we can draw the following provisional conclusions:

1. A-thinking makes it possible to begin teaching and learning history before the emergence of operational R-thinking at age 7-8. It is in fact well suited to the 'intuitive' stage; oral stories, fables and books are not only permissible at this stage, they are essential material for development.

2. Historical material contributes much to the general development of A-thinking in children (A^1, A^2, A^3), which as we have seen is both itself an effective method of thinking and a necessary seed-bed for R-thinking.

3. Hudson's evidence suggests that students taught associatively may make good historians.

4. History is a subject which nicely combines A and R elements in the suggestion of problem-solving strategies for past human situations. It therefore provides models or schema for similar strategies in present human situations.

History and adult thinking

Most historians, like other subject-teachers, believe that their subject is not simply a collection of facts relevant to examinations, but an intellectual discipline relevant to the conduct of life, and a long list of successful statesmen, diplomats, administrators and business men who have been historians lends somewhat unscientific support to their view. But there has been little attempt to describe the nature of this discipline. It is not enough to refer to the intrinsic demands of the subject—meticulous research, respect for the evidence, balanced judgment and so on—because these are attributes of any academic discipline. We must ask what the study of history can do which a thorough study of French or chemistry or philosophy cannot. Some general answers to this question are considered in Chapter 3. The present chapter is concerned with cognitive development, with the ways in which history may help a man to think more effectively.

The contention that history teaches us how to deal with present human situations has always been countered by the argument that history does not repeat itself, that no two human situations are alike. But this is too simple an account of the matter. What is in question is the process of transfer. Most psychologists of learning would accept that human minds normally develop concepts (strategies, schemata, learning sets) which are not limited in application to a single situation or problem, but are sufficiently generalized to be transferable to a range of other situations having some similarity to the original.

We are not primarily concerned whether a trained archaeologist is likely to give a better than average account of a road accident, or whether a documentary historian will make an above average evaluation of legal evidence, though these may well be the case. We are interested in the broader question whether, other things being equal, the historian, or the child who has learned history, is likely to be able to cope in an above-average way with a range of non-specific human situations. We could put this in a different way by asking whether learning history contributes to the development of intelligence.

The research on this question has still to be done, but we can suggest a number of areas which seem promising fields of inquiry:

1. *Transfer*. Generally speaking, school subjects are not taught for vocational purposes; most school leavers get jobs only marginally related to the specific content of their education. Nor are subjects taught for 'general knowledge': much of the knowledge is relevant only to quiz games. The subjects are taught on the unexpressed but probably justified assumption that they provide a 'discipline', that is, that there is some kind of conceptual transfer from each school subject to the business of adult life. But the research evidence suggests that if the gap between the learned material and the new situation is too great, the concept may either be forgotten, or retained but not seen as applicable to the new situation. Transfer is most likely to take place if the learner is introduced to the new situation in the process of directed or guided discovery in which the gaps are kept small. Our argument is that there is too great a gap between the strategies acquired in many school subjects and the situations of adult life, so that transfer is less effective than it might be. Schools, colleges and universities should therefore have specific programmes for effecting transfer. We have argued elsewhere that environmental studies provide one such programme; history, in which the student of languages or chemistry can apply his learned strategies in the analysis of human situations, is another.

2. *Concreteness*. A particular aspect of the problem of transfer is the transition from abstraction to concreteness. Part of the business of education is necessarily the progressive abstraction of the material, its reduction to a system of symbols which can then be logically manipulated. But the problem is that when we come to transfer these logical abilities to the business of adult life, it is very much more difficult to abstract the symbols from the material. The material appears in the concrete form of people, places, institutions, social groups—the confusing kaleidoscope of human society. This is almost a percep-

tual rather than a cognitive problem: logical relationships which have been seen in two-dimensions, in black-and-white, on a page, on a blackboard, in a diagram, or which have been contained in a test-tube or on a dissecting table, have now to be seen in colour, in constant movement, in three dimensions, and subject to incessant change. It is not surprising that in trying to cope with the everyday world, school leavers regress to a concrete operational or even pre-operational mode of thinking, and that A-thinking proves to be surprisingly common in adult life. There is a general argument, then, for the teaching of material about people and places, that is the humane studies, as a necessary auxiliary to other disciplines. But there is a particular argument for the teaching of history, which has throughout the school been concerned with the refinement of A-thinking, with the use of imagery and association in the analysis of human affairs, and in the effective synthesis of A and R-thinking.

3. *Creativity*. If, as has been argued, creativity or originality is related to the effective use of the random products of A-thinking, then history, which by the very nature of its material makes use of imagery and association in the process of analysis, provides a training in creative thinking. This training must of course be transferred or guided into other fields; what is proposed, for instance, is that a good history/sociology graduate, or a good historian, retrained as a sociologist, is likely to have above-average originality as a sociologist.

4. *Divergence*. Discussions of convergence/divergence (Hudson, 1966) frequently lead to the conclusion that formal education produces too many convergers and not enough divergers. How then should the school set about the development of divergent thinking? Hudson's evidence showed that divergers tended to be historians. It is, of course, relevant to our argument that divergence is a quality useful to historians, and also that diverger-his-

torians were not particularly outstanding in normal R-thinking intelligence tests. What is more interesting is the possibility that teaching history actually produces divergers: and this is consonant with our view of the nature of the subject. On the one hand, history makes use of A-thinking, which throws up absurd, humorous and colourful associations of a divergent type. On the other hand, history is a subject in which it is difficult to assemble all the evidence, difficult to have conclusive proof, and yet easy to find, from the vast range of material, rival evidence or a different argument; it is a subject therefore which encourages and respects divergent interpretations.

5. *Probability*. Bruner and several other commentators have discussed the inability of students to use probabilistic reasoning, a mode of thinking important both in mathematics and science, and in the analysis of social problems. It has been suggested that the formal school subjects of Western education have habituated students to certainty reasoning, and that the curriculum should include more material requiring a probabilistic approach (Bruner, 1956, p. 181). When badly taught, of course, history takes on the character of certainty, but essentially history is a study of uncertainties and likelihoods, and when well taught, develops in its students a probabilistic frame of mind.

6. *Analogies*. The function of analogies in creative thinking has been discussed by many writers. The suggestion of analogies is clearly one of the products of A-thinking, and the place of history in developing and making use of A-thinking has already been considered. But, in addition, history makes use of analogy at every level of its activity, from the interpretation of an obscure manuscript by analogy with the known text of another, to the comparative study of revolutions or of the imperial policies of Rome and Great Britain. Indeed, the often discussed relationship of historical events to the problems of the present day is that of analogy rather than example. And

history as a discipline is itself very responsive to modification by analogy. An era of landownership was associated with an interest in genealogy and feudal England; an industrial society with the Marxist interpretation and the development of social and economic history; the appearance of a professional civil service with administrative history; the population explosion with historical demography; analytical philosophy with professional history. A historical training, then, is more likely to encourage the use of analogy than many others.

7. *Judgment.* It has been suggested elsewhere that the use of cognitive skills in everyday adult life may be more properly described as 'judgment' than as 'intelligence' (Watts, 1969, p. 68; Watts, 1971). 'Judgment' appears to be a battery of skills which includes some sensori-motor elements; relevant perceptual skills; more familiarity with concrete situations than the school provides; A-thinking as well as R-thinking; the use of imagery, guesses and hunches; and ability in probabilistic reasoning. In the Platonic tradition, abstract thinking is often confused with effective thinking, but in fact many tasks of adult life may be performed more effectively if thinking at least partially regresses to more 'primitive' forms (McKellar, 1968, p. 113). History, by the very nature of its material, already makes use of such a state of 'regression'.

Conclusion

This chapter has been concerned with the interrelationship between the process of cognitive development from infancy to adulthood, and the learning of history. A view of cognitive development has been advanced which enables us to suggest the following conclusions:

1. The cognitive structures of infants are effective enough to deal with at least some concepts of a historical character. It is not of course being suggested that history

39

should be 'taught' by the imposition of abstract material, but that children should, indeed must, be given the opportunity to elaborate their conceptual abilities through historical material.

2. It is important that children should have the opportunity to develop not only what we have called the A-thinking of the expressive arts or the R-thinking of logico-mathematical reasoning, but the AR thinking of history and other humane subjects. Not to do so in the school would be to disadvantage the working-class child.

3. The historical frame of mind, the kind of responding and thinking which develops during the study of the past activities of human beings, does seem to be made up of concepts and strategies which can be readily transferred to other fields of academic enquiry and to the problems of adult life.

3

What is history?

There have been many attempts to define 'history'. We can begin this particular discussion by making a distinction between (1) history as what actually happened in the past; (2) history as our inevitably imperfect understanding of what happened in the past and (3) history as the continuing attempt by professional historians to extend our knowledge and improve our understanding of what happened in the past (Marwick, 1970, p. 17). If we look carefully at these three statements, it is evident that none of them imply that history has an existence in itself, as a corpus of knowledge and opinion embodied in books and evidence. History is being defined in dynamic terms, in (1) as a series of occurrences, in (2) as a state of understanding, and in (3) as a process of research. We are thus taking an inter-actionist view: that history cannot exist as a book on a shelf, but only as a process of interaction between historical material and the people involved with it (Watts, 1969, p. 21 sq.; Dewey, 1916, p. 158 sq.; Collingwood, 1946, p. 248).

If we ask who are the participants in (2), the answer must be not the few specialists on each historical topic, but the interested non-specialist public, which includes historians outside their own specialisms. It seems to me that professional historians writing about their subject jump from (1) the material, to (3) the research, without giving adequate consideration to (2) the general understanding, and so mistakenly try to define as 'history' the professional activity of contributing to this general understanding. I have discussed elsewhere the difficulty of defining educational objectives in terms of a minority concern (1969, pp. 13-14). There may, of course, be some strictly academic goals which have reference only to a minority, but *educational* objectives must start from propositions about what most ordinary people actually do, or what they could reasonably be expected to do with the best available teaching methods.

This reference to 'doing' takes us to another threefold distinction, between history defined in terms of its content, history defined in terms of its techniques and history defined in terms of response. Apart perhaps from some Marxists, few historians now attempt to define history in terms of some required *content*: as an account of national development, perhaps, or of progress, or of the rise of democracy, or of the class struggle (Huizinga, 1956, pp. 294-6; Elton, 1967, p. 42; but see Carr, 1961; Plumb, 1964). Such definitions are still sometimes embodied in suggested curricula—'progress' and 'democracy', for instance, are treated as key concepts in some American schemes—but the results look distinctly old-fashioned (Gomez, 1968, p. 179). Professional historians, on the other hand, are inclined to define history in terms of *technique*, in terms of meticulous scholarship, professionalism, scholarly standards and so forth (Elton, 1967, pp. 86-7, 182) and this has influenced some modern approaches to the history curriculum. A Schools Council booklet (1969), for instance, defines history as 'an investigation, an observation of the facts, an examination of evidence'. But if we look carefully at these propositions, it becomes clear that they could equally be applied to any scholarly discipline. *All* disciplines require (or embody in their teaching) a rigorous, objective, exhaustive examination of their particular materials, so that 'historical' techniques are also used by logicians, philosophers, lawyers and physicists. This does not help us in our attempt to distinguish what it is that is truly historical.

I propose here to develop a definition in terms of *response*: to say that history is that to which people respond historically, and that a historical response is an emotional or intellectual reaction to the knowledge, or the belief, that certain things were so in the past. Such a response is what Trevor-Roper calls 'a sense of the past ... the first qualification of an historian' (1971, p. 227). We should distinguish a historical response from the artistic response which we experience in fiction, drama, poetry and the like. Our response to these involves a suspension of disbelief and an acceptance of the creative personal view of the artist. In history, our response is grounded on reality; we must suppose that the events occurred, and be satisfied with the evidence that they did so. There are, of course, greater and lesser degrees of validity in such responses. If, for example, on reading a popular textbook we come to believe that two-thirds of the population died in the Black Death, we may experience a historical response, though one of rather low validity; if we do some research on manorial records and find that of twenty named tenants in a rent roll of 1346, fifteen are described as dead in a court roll of 1349, we also experience a historical response, but one of greater validity.

Such a definition of history in terms of response to real past events puts us into a position to find an answer to some of the apparent problems of the subject. It makes it possible, for instance, to give a place to the vast area of popular history, which shades off into historical fiction, folk-lore and even day-dreaming. It enables us to see the responses of small children to, say, the death of Bede, as genuinely historical, and to describe the teaching/learning process in terms of a slow progression from history of low validity to history of high validity. And this is consonant with our interpretation of the psychology of learning history in Chapter 2. We can note that 'Responding' is one of the categories of objectives in Bloom's affective domain (Krathwohl, *et al.*, 1964).

The subject cannot be satisfactorily defined in terms of the productions of professional historians (Trevor-Roper, 1957). We must involve in a concept of 'history' all the people who 'make' history in a different sense from writing it. There are historical producers and historical consumers, and no special virtue in being on one or the other. In fact there may be many sensitive consumers whose depth of response to historical material is greater than that of the industrious historical journeyman who presents it. It is not always the editor of a collection of letters or papers who makes the best use of the material: indeed, it is precisely the function of the rules of historical scholarship that this should be so. And it is arguable that some professional writings are merely the intelligent exercise of analysis on historical material, and not history at all, for they lack a sense of the past.

Historical consumers are the people (including of course producers) who have a historical response or experience from an encounter with properly presented historical material, and in Britain, they probably form a majority of the population. Historical producers are those who professionally devote themselves to validating historical material, improving its presentation and discovering new material. They include researchers, writers of histories, creative lecturers, archivists and others. Between the two is an important class of historical merchants, the translaters, whose business it is to stimulate demand by showing people what a historical experience can be, and to find ways of presenting the sometimes arcane products of the professional historians to a wider public. These merchants include lecturers, teachers, publishers, popular historians, writers of textbooks, librarians, and television, radio and film producers. The point to be made here is that production, translation and consumption are different, and equally, reputable ways of handling historical material, and that the house rules of production ought not (and indeed cannot) be made to dictate the nature of the other two processes, which have their own characteristics and standards.

A response definition, then, allows us to envisage historical education as any educative process must be conceived, as something applicable to a majority of ordinary people. History becomes merely an esoteric activity if it does not play a part in refining the experience of the man-in-the-street: we should not try to define a historical education primarily in terms of the apprenticeship of professional historians (though this is an important secondary goal which good teachers will keep in mind). And we need not doubt the purpose of teaching history to children who are never going to be historians, nor suppose that classroom activities necessarily have to be made into simplified versions of professional techniques.

Our definition enables us to include in a discussion of the nature of the subject a great range of popular writing, producing, drama and art which is already in common usage described as history; it also helps us to clarify the extent to which historians are involved in the process of communication (Marwick, 1970, p. 142 sq.). An historical response may of course properly remain a personal and unshared experience, even when it has broadened into a response to a major historical theme. But part of a response is likely to be the wish to share it, which is expressed, in one form, as historical writing, and we know that large numbers of ordinary people are a potential

45

audience for such communication. Most historians, in spite of the influence of narrow theories on the nature of their subject, have in fact written as though this might be so. Historical writing, at least in Britain, has remained refreshingly free from the jargon and pretentious obscurity which has afflicted some other academic disciplines. Very few historical works are published which cannot be read with interest by a competent sixth-former; probably the majority can reasonably be recommended to a keen class in adult education, and some historians of the first rank —Trevor-Roper, Alan Bullock, A. J. P. Taylor, Asa Briggs, W. G. Hoskins—can attract mass audiences both for their writings and for their radio and television work. All this suggests that the response definition is operationally a sound one.

Such historians of course reveal two capacities: a capacity to produce good professional history, and a capacity to communicate their response to history. In other words, we can distinguish the process of research from the process of reflecting historically upon it. In practice, the two processes take place together: a historian is already reflecting on his material when he chooses a subject and identifies his sources. But they are nevertheless different processes, and an interest in the skilled activities of production should not obscure the fact that the key to the whole activity is in the reflection. It is the quality of reflection which distinguishes a great historian from a good historian. Maitland from Oman, or Namier from Trevelyan.

When we try to analyse what constitutes quality of historical reflection, we are obviously at the nub of the subject, and it would be impossible in a book such as this to do more than sketch out some approaches to an answer. We may begin generally by suggesting that this quality has three constituents: general intelligence, historical intelligence and historical 'intuition'. *General in-*

telligence of course comprises those cognitive skills, of analysis, synthesis and so on, which could be equally well applied to any other intellectual activity. Within *historical intelligence*, we can include cognitive skills such as a sense of time, tolerance of ambiguity and creativity, which though general are abnormally developed by continuous acquaintance with historical material. By *historical intuition*, we mean those cognitive and affective skills which can *only* be fully developed and utilized in the context of historical material or some closely associated field of study. In Namier's words, 'the crowning attainment of historical study is an historical sense ... the final conclusions ... are intuitive' (1956, pp. 375, 379).

The great historian employs groups of these various skills in different ways. One group of skills is employed in setting up a comprehensive, multi-dimensional dynamic model of men and society at a particular period, in which all the features known to contemporary scholarship are given due place; features which may range perhaps from the illness of a major figure to vernacular architecture and to price and population statistics. The model may either actually be set out in the historian's work; or his command of it may be only implicit in the sensitive handling of his edition of a charter or a letter. Second, within the model, the historian uses another group of skills to spotlight, or throw into relief, certain features which, the reader is persuaded, really were the more significant factors in the society and events of the period. Third, by a combination of sympathy and objectivity, the historian allows the personality of his characters and the nature of society to stand forth in a way which, we feel, does justice to them in terms of their own time.

Objectives

The previous paragraph could be interpreted in terms of

47

the categories from Bloom's well-known *Taxonomy of Educational Objectives*: that is, we could say that the historian is concerned (among other things) with comprehension and extrapolation, with synthesis, with analysis, and with evaluation (Bloom *et al.*, 1956). But useful though Bloom's book is, this labelling does not get us very far. For Bloom's analysis is made on the premise that there is a hierarchy of cognitive processes common to thinking about all relatively difficult topics, processes which if they take place efficiently may be called 'intelligence'. His analysis does help us in constructing teaching materials which permit the exercise and encourage the development of these cognitive processes, and in devising evaluative procedures to test for them; it is useful to see historical material in terms of the categories knowledge, comprehension, analysis, synthesis and evaluation and their subcategories. But if we go on to take Bloom's taxonomy as not merely descriptive of some aspects of our subject, but prescriptive of what material we ought to include, we may find that we are treating history like all other subjects namely, as classes of material contributing to 'cognitive development'. We are, of course, interested in cognitive development in Chapter 4, but we are concerned here with *history*, and what is distinctive—not common —in history's contribution to learning. And Bloom's contributors are not helpful in that area; a glance at the examples and at the specimen questions shows that those which incorporate historical material are few and historically naïve (Jones, 1970a, p. 60; Jones, 1970b; Carpenter, 1964, p. 27).

Further, the application of modern conceptions of curriculum development to history has been made difficult by the fact that there are no 'law' concepts in history (Huizinga, 1956, p. 290). There are 'fact' concepts of varying degrees of generality, ranging from 'William of Normandy invaded England in 1066' to 'control of London was an important factor in the success of Parliament in the first stages of the Civil War'. And there are broad 'circumscribing concepts' implicit in the nature of historical subject-matter—that it is bound by the nature of time, the life-span of human beings and so on (see p. 51). But the attempts of writers like Hegel, Marx, Spengler and Toynbee to discern 'law' concepts in history are now generally considered to be unhistorical (Elton, 1967, p. 42). So that sequential and hierarchical structures of knowledge, building up from lower-order to higher-order principles, which are very useful in analysing learning in mathematics, the sciences, languages and some of the social sciences (see Gagné, 1965), are simply not relevant to history (we may of course be able to teach associated historical techniques such as languages or statistics in a structured way, and this may be a useful part of the training of professional historians).

On the other hand, the concept of a *spiral curriculum* is a useful one in history (Bruner, 1960, p. 52 sq.). This notion assumes that the relatively small number of key concepts of any subject can be introduced in a simplified form at a low level of understanding, and then reintroduced at deepening levels of understanding as the syllabus develops. We are thus able to consider the circumscribing concepts described below as forming such key concepts, introduced in the earliest historical stories and reappearing in more sophisticated forms at the various levels of historical learning.

The absence of sequential development in historical learning does not, of course, make history an inferior subject to those subjects like science which do involve such development; it is merely a different subject, with different teaching problems. But unwillingness to accept this absence has contributed to sad failures in some modern approaches to the history curriculum, and more seriously, to the failure of much traditional history teaching in

49

schools. For teachers have believed that a chronological sequence is the same as a learning sequence; that by teaching children about the Tudors last year, the Stuarts this year and the Industrial Revolution next year, the children's understanding would be improved—whereas all they were doing was learning blocks of historical fact set end to end. Even university syllabuses show signs of this weakness, though it may be excused by some unconvincing propositions about 'broad' or 'narrow' courses and 'good solid work'.

The concepts of history are not, then, as they may be in mathematics or physics, summary statements of central features of the material itself. In history, no part of the material is central. We may write or teach very proper history—and no other history at all—even if we confine ourselves to the history of Piddletrenthide, Puerto Rico, the London Goldsmiths or the office of Lord Privy Seal (Huizinga, 1956, p. 300). Neither wars nor politics nor wages, crises, turning-points or revolutions are essential to history, though they may be included in it. The extreme case to consider is the refugee Tibetan historian, quite ignorant of all history outside that of his own religion and people, who may, I suggest, still feel instantly at home in a company of Western historians. What characterizes history is the treatment of material from man's past in a historical way; we can agree with the Schools Council's proposition that 'what makes subject matter historical is the way it is studied' (1969, p. 14). We may write, teach and learn good history about Piddletrenthide as long as material for its history survives in sufficient quantity for all the characteristic features of history to emerge. Our task here is to define those features so that they can be embodied in the selection of material for a curriculum at any level.

Characteristics and concepts

To recapitulate, I have argued that history is that to which people respond historically; that a historical response is an emotional or intellectual reaction to the knowledge or the belief that certain things were so in the past; and that we must suppose that the events occurred, and be satisfied with the evidence that they did so. And I have suggested that this definition implies some 'circumscribing concepts' which make history distinctive not merely because it is about the past, but because we have to think in characteristic ways about it.

History lies in the debatable land between the arts and the sciences. The basic mode of history, the historical response, is akin to an aesthetic experience (Marwick, 1970, p. 14). Yet history is not, like the arts, a truth-creating activity: it is a science in that it is a truth-seeking activity. A response can only be truly historical if we are satisfied with the truth of the material. History however is a science working with material which can never be seen in its original state. History cannot experiment or repeat experiments, question the authors of its evidence, seek eye-witnesses, survey, measure and so on. Even its discovery of new evidence is essentially fortuitous. Though history must wring out every ounce of meaning from it, its evidence is ultimately intractable and sphinx-like. History then has a distinctive relationship with *evidence*, and it is a circumscribing concept of 'pure' history that it must show an awareness of evidence as part of its sense of the past (Elton, 1967, p. 87). And to apply this to the schools, questions of evidence—'do we really know?' and 'how do we know?'—can be raised almost from the beginning of children's acquaintance with historical material.

A second characteristic which arises out of the nature of the evidence is *uncertainty*. Most academic subjects would claim that their evidence is less certain than it appears to be to the layman. But none can be quite so bedevilled by inadequate and untestable evidence as history, in which pieces of evidence of greater or less uncertainty prop one another up like packs of cards into narrative accounts or analytical schemes. Elton rightly points out that this aspect of history can be exaggerated (ibid., p. 79 sq.). Much historical material has a high degree of probability; the accumulated evidence persuades me, for instance, that I can be almost as certain that William of Normandy invaded England in the autumn of the year 1066 as that German aircraft attacked parts of southern England in the summer of 1940, an event which I experienced. But it remains true, as we saw in Chapter 2, that most historical reasoning can be described as 'probabilistic', and that this is arguably one of the strengths of history as an intellectual discipline (Bloch, 1954, pp. 124-5). Uncertainty is a key concept of history which has often been omitted in school history teaching.

History, like Milton's Paradise, is bound to seem dull if everything is predetermined. We should always be prepared to say that we are 'not sure' in our assessment of evidence and in our historical judgments, to admit that many historical 'facts' have only a probability of 0·6. But uncertainty is also part of history in a different sense from the inadequacy of evidence. We have to accept the uncertainty of the course of history itself, in the play of the contingent, the trivial and the accidental. 'Only by recognising that the possibilities are unlimited can the historian do justice to the fulness of life' (Huizinga, 1956, p. 192; Bloch, 1954). In the school, children readily understand the implications of the story of the horseshoe nail, and the parable of Cleopatra's nose seldom fails to arouse an appreciative chuckle (see Carr, 1961, pp. 94-5).

The uncertainty of history implies another essential characteristic, that it is a subject of *debate*, not of authority, of interpretation rather than judgment, that it is necessary to be critically aware of the extent to which history is the opinion of historians. We can recognize the danger which Elton points to (Elton, 1967, p. 181), that in college courses students may be invited to discuss historiography without actually having done any history (this is a danger which the Open University Humanities Foundation Course may run). But it nevertheless remains true that historiography, the study of the writing of history, must go hand in hand with the study of historical topics. And this can be done in the school. Children will readily identify discrepancies and differences of emphasis in a pair of textbooks. More generally, they are naturally ready to see two sides to a question in historical themes; it is not difficult to organize pieces of writing, drama, and role-playing about the Greeks and the Persians, the Romans and Britons, or Roundheads and Cavaliers.

History is about the past activities of human beings, and so is about *people*, people as individuals and people in groups. Elton is doubtful whether biography is history at all; but this doubt seems to me merely part of his intelligent but essentially conservative attempt to justify the kind of historical topics he is accustomed to teaching (Elton, 1967, p. 169). The study of an individual's response to historical circumstances would appear to be as valid a form of history as the study of the responses of large or small groups. At least we can agree that history is essentially not about things, as are perhaps archaeology, industrial archaeology, architectural history, geology and some kinds of historical geography. The most difficult borderline here is in the relationship between man and material things in social and economic history. The clue in this case is to keep men in the picture, both literally and metaphorically. We should show clothes with people in them, machines being used, weapons wielded in battle: or we risk teaching not history but the fascinating and unhistorical antiquarianism of *Jane's Fighting Ships*.

History is not about things; nor, on the other hand, is it about abstractions (Huizinga, 1956, p. 298). It is about people involved in particular, unique events (Marwick *et al.*, 1970, p. 24). History is not a discipline which develops from the concrete to the abstract, but from a simple understanding of the concrete to a more sophisticated understanding of the concrete. Abstractions may be the proper concern of a theologian who wants to discuss fate or retribution in an historical context, of a philosopher who discusses the nature of knowledge in relation to history, or of a sociologist who gives a historical dimension to an analytical concept such as socialization. But they are not history. The trouble with Marxist history, for instance, is not so much what it says as that it so fills historical rooms with theoretical lumber that we find it difficult to imagine anyone really living there.

School history has always concerned itself with people and with events; in this respect the modern *Ladybird* books continue a tradition of story-telling which we can find in Day's *Sandford and Merton* written in the 1780s. Barraclough's criticism of 'mulling over Simon de Montfort for ever' could hardly be more inappropriate to most school teaching. The traditional material can of course be well or badly taught. But this is no reason why we should not introduce children in the junior school to Simon de Montfort, and to Charlemagne and Peter the Great and Abraham Lincoln, in the reasonable expectation that when they are older, the children will come to have a deeper understanding of these people and the events in which they were involved. In the place they give to people, the schools in fact reflect some of the best features of recent historical scholarship—Powicke's work on Simon de Montfort and Edward I, Neale's work on Elizabeth, Wedgwood's on Charles I, Namier's on the eighteenth-century aristocracy.

We should certainly be on our guard in school history against the impersonal abstraction—monasticism, feudalism, industrialization and the like. But there is also an indeterminate area which has its dangers—the impersonal person: The Norman knight, The Puritan preacher, The village labourer. Such representative figures should wherever possible be real people from the past, found in the evidence; if not, they should be fictitious people given names and characters. The merely impersonal persons are the Rosencrantz and Guildenstern's of the historical scene; not only are they the puppet-like creations of the author, they are very difficult for children to conceptualize.

Because history is about men, it is also about *change* (Elton, 1967, p. 22). This is one key concept which has justifiably been picked out in a number of curriculum projects (Schools Council, 1969). But simply to put into the curriculum a topic called 'Change in the twentieth century' is too crude an application of the concept. *Change* is, as it were, the language of history, in which *events* are the words and *narrative* the sentences. What we should be concerned with is that school history topics should be dynamic, not frozen at a moment in time. We can thus identify some of the weaknesses in traditional history teaching, and to see the danger in the more modern 'patch' approach. One topic which has perhaps suffered most from an over-static treatment is 'the Romans', who would appear in some school histories to have landed in Kent in A.D. 45 and to have left again in A.D. 410 unaffected by four hundred years of experience; with one result that older students are led into mis-statements about the slowly-changing nature of Roman society. Less obvious, but perhaps more serious in its distortion of English history, is 'the Anglo-Saxon peasant', a concept requiring as it does the telescoping of six hundred years of development. And this peasant goes straight on into 'the medieval village', beloved of generations of visual aid suppliers, which supposedly continued in its tediously conservative way until abolished by those gentlemen-inclosers of the eighteenth century. Something similar seems to have happened to 'the medieval monastery', 'the feudal system' and 'the Industrial Revolution' (when did it end?). Some simplification in history is of course necessary, and is discussed below. But it is not difficult to choose details to suggest change, to show in illustrations for instance a ruined old building and a half-built new one, or to include in stories a reminiscent grandfather and an enterprising grandson.

The over-static picture is also a problem for museums. The bigger museums do have the resources to show progressive change in a series of objects, and even to mount animated displays; but smaller museums in particular may rely on a scene of 'A cottage interior of Wordsworth's time', which only confirms a static textbook account of the eighteenth-century peasant. And we can see in this context the value of fieldwork, in which the eighteenth-century almshouses really do stand between the nineteenth-century brewery and the new supermarket.

History is about people and about change, and so it is also about *time*—time, that is, in the specifically historical sense. In Bloch's words, 'human time will never conform to the implacable uniformity and fixed divisions of clock time' (1954, pp. 27-9, 189). Some previous discussions of this subject have been bedevilled by a tendency to confuse clock and calendar time with historical time (McKellar, 1968, p. 175). In my view, these two concepts, though related, each require quite a different conceptual apparatus, so that a child with a ready understanding of clock time may be immature in his grasp of historical time, and vice versa. Historical time, the recognition that human beings exist in a time dimension as a series of generations of which ours is the most recent, is a much more profound concept than the ability to organize daily life around clocks and calendars. Historical material has, of course, an important role to play in developing this concept. A first step, and one which comes quite easily to young children with their ready understanding of the roles of grand-parents, parents and children, is generational time, a recognition that this generation's parents are next generation's grandparents, this generation's children are next generation's parents, and so on. Elementary genealogical games with great-great-great-great grandparents, and the easily understandable descent of the present Queen from Queen Victoria, are helpful illustrations here. Still more helpful in placing major events in a generational context are historical novels like *Children of the New Forest*, in which children grow up in one regime, have adventures in another, and marry and settle down in a third. We can show that Oliver Cromwell was a little boy when Elizabeth died; and that a London boy born on the day Charles I was executed would have been ten when he stood in the crowd to cheer the restored Charles II.

The teacher has of course to be alert to the age-range he is teaching, and to modify his presentation of changing time to take account of it. Infants, juniors, adolescents, young and middle-aged adults stretch and concertina time to take account of their place in it and of their own experience. And it does not follow that age automatically brings a more subtle understanding of time. One of the problems of the adult learner, with several uneventful decades of life behind him, is a tendency to dismiss historical decades in a cursory phrase. He too needs an awareness of the rich texture of history to be helped to put events in perspective. It is particularly important to be able to see remote and lesser-known historical periods in a familiar time setting. We can note for instance that the Dark Age between the Anglo-Saxon invasions and the landing of St Augustine of Canterbury was as long as the crowded period since James Watt sat and watched a boiling kettle.

But history is not just about the way people grow up

and pass through different social roles. It is also about the way in which *people change in time* as individuals—the essential biographical element in history (Pares, 1961, p. 7). People grow up and mature, age and die and in the process they contribute to and are changed by the people and events with which they are involved. Richard II, a courageous boy, can be seen growing middle-aged and neurotic; Elizabeth, a lonely and frightened girl, becomes an irascible old woman; Charles I, a spoilt and priggish youth, achieves nobility at Whitehall. Where the evidence exists, it is the business of the historian at any level to give an account of these changes, to interpret and evaluate them. That most of the people for whom enough evidence exists are Famous People, and that we have less opportunity to glimpse the man-in-the-street of any era, is perhaps a pity, but it is not an excuse for neglecting the familiar stories.

We must be alert, however, to the dangers of the biographical method, and take care that our historical characters do not remain stage figures. Henry V, with his rebellious youth and noble manhood, who has had both the advantage and the disadvantage of receiving splendid treatment from Shakespeare and Olivier, is a case in point. His life and career needs to be exposed to the questioning, debate, interpretation and evaluation we have already discussed. So too do Drake and Marlborough, Florence Nightingale and Winston Churchill. Obviously, though, there have to be degrees of sophistication in our accounts of maturation. In the lower school, we may be content with a simple two or three stage account, based on some portraits or, for example, on the coins and stamps of Victoria. But in the secondary school we can be more ambitious (see p. 81).

In the modern period, photographs and documentary film make possible graphic accounts of the maturation and ageing of individuals; the few well-chosen photographs of Asquith in Roy Jenkins's biography, for instance, seem to me a particularly poignant example (Jenkins, 1964). Indeed, we are now able to do something like this even for the man-in-the-street. Children can be encouraged to make use of their own family photograph albums, and with a suitable photocopier (and family permission) enough material may be compiled for a variety of projects. And anonymous photograph albums, otherwise worthless and picked up for a few pence in junk shops, sometimes give a more moving impression of the passage of families through time than photographs of people we know well.

History is not only about individuals changing in time; it is also about *groups of people changing in time*, groups of all sizes, married couples like Victoria and Albert, parents and children like Randolph and Winston Churchill, families of all sizes, communities, nations, social classes, religious communities and racial groups. But there are some dangers here too. We make the assumption, an essentially sociological one, that all social groups have structures and shared experiences which make it meaningful to talk about the history of the group rather than of the individuals that make it up. And this assumption, though it may seem validated by common-sense experience, needs looking at a little more carefully. In my view, this is an area in which historians may in the future benefit most from the application of sociological methods and concepts. To talk about a formal organization like the Roman army is safe enough, but it is not so safe to talk about the feudal aristocracy or the Elizabethan gentry. One of the ways in which historians have caused themselves most trouble—and created bad school history—is in the virtual invention of groups which in fact had no common structure and therefore no identity. The working-class is perhaps the best-known of these non-groups. *The Making of the English Working Class* is the title of a very well known work (Thompson, 1963), but it may be doubted whether the 'working-class' ever existed as a definable group and whether it could be 'made'. Groups of working people with shared experiences, in urban and rural communities, in occupational groups and in particular work-places, undoubtedly existed and have fascinating histories. And we may, by looking at census returns or price statistics, be able to make some generalized points which illustrate the lives of them all. But whether we can talk about them as though they were all capable of common responses is very much more doubtful.

There is a rather similar danger in the excessively topographical approach to local history, in the presumption that anything which has a proper name and a boundary around it must have a history worth writing. Many tedious county, town and parish histories have been written on the assumption that a description of the events which occurred within their boundaries amounts to history. The real historical problem, in fact, is often the identification of the actual social groups existing in and around an administrative location.

But with these words of caution in mind, the teacher can still find social groups and genuine communities of all kinds on which his class may work. He could begin with family history and genealogy, starting in the lower school with imaginary families, the children's own families and the royal family, with upper juniors going on the local families as they appear in parish registers, or in the case of gentry families, in the pages of local histories (Steel and Taylor, 1969, 1971). Local family history leads us in one direction into the history of the people who made up the local community, to the parish chest and the local newspaper, and can be illustrated by the finding of local field-work. It may also lead us outwards to link up with the royal family through the histories of influential noble families like the Russells and the Howards. And thence we may find ourselves returning, with a clearer understanding, to the traditional narrative history of political groups, parliaments and governments.

Pure and applied history

This chapter has been an attempt to delineate what we mean by history itself, and to see how such a concept of history can be related to a school curriculum. But schools are not concerned only with the objectives of 'subjects'; they also use the material of subjects in the pursuit of quite different objectives. We can make the distinction in the terms 'pure' and 'applied' history.

This distinction is not intended as a tendentious one: no chaste virtue is implied by 'pure' nor wise practicality by 'applied'. It simply serves to indicate that the material of history—ideas and evidence about the past activities of human beings—like any other intellectual material, can either be looked at simply for what it is, as one self-justifying area of human experience, or can be seen as making a contribution to some other area, to growing up, for instance, to learning a job, or getting a degree. Clearly, when we are doing any kind of history at all, we are nearly always contributing to both pure and applied history, and when we are deeply involved in a real piece of history it may seem a barren exercise to analyse what we are concerned with. But in undertaking work in history—in planning a curriculum, for instance, or compiling a reading list—the distinction between pure and applied has to be made; for although we may be dealing with the same material, each approach may require this material to be differently structured and interpreted. Chapter 4, then, goes on to discuss various forms of applied history, and their application in the school.

Pure history is the reading or studying of history simply for the sake of doing so, because, like Everest, it is there. All manifestations of human behaviour, from mountaineering to water-skiing and keeping cats, have this capacity of engrossing some one of us. But some interests are more powerful and persuasive than others, and history is one of these. We could put this in a slightly different way, and say that history is a powerful form of curiosity. Curiosity appears to be an innate characteristic of living things—we have a tendency to orientate ourselves to stimuli, to satisfy ourselves about the unknown; rats will explore mazes without the lure of a reward (Gabriel, 1968, p. 152). In academic studies, this curiosity is disciplined; it is deliberately confined to a certain area of knowledge, and it proceeds by accepted rules and with the aid of practised techniques. All academic disciplines can be described as disciplined curiosity within a given area of knowledge; in the case of history within our knowledge of the past activities of men. And looked at differently again, pure history is a form of aesthetic experience; we have a profound feeling of satisfaction, beauty, or *catharsis* from the contemplation of all or part of the historical process, just as we have from music or poetry or looking at a picture. This experience is autonomous, it does not have to relate to some other objective; this is the aesthetic component of 'the historical response' or the 'sense of the past'.

4

History applied

Applied history is history used for some purpose other than knowing history or responding historically; its forms may range from the ridiculous (in supplying questions for quiz games), to the sublime (providing plots for Shakespeare's plays). As we have noticed, there is no necessary dichotomy between it and pure history; in many areas the two approaches overlap. But in this chapter I shall try to isolate some of history's applications. In the context of the school, I shall identify three general themes: integration, socialization and personal development.

Integration

History lends itself readily to illustrating and supporting other subjects. It is an important element of environmental studies in the locality, and of integrated studies of other lands, and it is nearly always part of project and topic work in the junior school. Religion is often most effectively approached in the school through history. The historical background is unavoidable in the Old and New Testaments, in the lives of saints, monks and missionaries; while men like Thomas More, George Fox and John Wesley illustrate dramatically the nature of religious commitment. If well-taught, a historical approach may provide, in the secondary school in particular, a point of contact with otherwise forbidding topics in mathematics and science. Art history is an important element in art education, musical history in music, and so on. History and literature, history and geography, history and modern languages— there are many familiar combinations at all levels of education in which history plays a useful supporting role.

Socialization

Important aspects of what sociologists call socialization are dealt with below under the heading of personal development. In this section, I am limiting the word to the child's preparation for the particular kind of public society in which he is brought up (Burston, 1963, p. 164). History plays an important part in this process, being used deliberately in some countries, and less consciously but just as effectively in Britain. The difficult questions of indoctrination involved cannot be argued out in a book of this kind. I shall simply assert, to establish a position, that until adolescence, in first and middle schools, teachers have a responsibility to convey a sense of sympthy with the kind of society in which the child lives. After adolescence, in the lower secondary school, the position should be reversed, and elements of contrast and criticism progressively introduced, incidentally applying to a social purpose one of the characteristics of pure history—debate—discussed above.

But whatever guide lines we suggest, it is certain that history curricula, textbooks, visual aids, even field work, will have socializing effects. Children learn that they are British (and English, Welsh and Scots and Irish); that many brave and attractive people have been British; that much history is concerned with the preservation of the British state; that Britain has played an important part in world affairs. They find that much blood has been shed to establish and defend a certain form of religion. They learn that Britain evolved a distinctive political system, and a pattern of central and local government, and that adults think it important that they should play a part in it. They learn that the League of Nations and the United Nations have tried to prevent wars, and so on. Much of this material may seem unexceptionable and hardly worth commenting on, but without history teaching, or with a different kind of history teaching, there is little doubt that social attitudes would be markedly different from those we are accustomed to.

Personal development

In this section we consider child-centred history, the use of historical material to help children to grow up, to mature, or to lead a fuller life. Though an argument has been advanced for the study of pure history in schools, many teachers may still prefer to think that child-centred history is the proper concept for the school. We can distinguish the *physical*, *intellectual* and *emotional* aspects of personal development. *Physical development* is a rather peripheral function of history teaching, but history provides good subjects for dance, drama, mime, charades and the like. Outside the school, history, as part of local studies, gives direction to an afternoon's walk, and is a normal feature of town trails and nature trails. A walking tour of hill forts or a cycle tour of parish churches are traditional English open-air activities, while the study of mines and quarries or the exploration of coastal sites by sail and canoe have their place in more rigorous outdoor pursuits courses. And one of the most attractive cheap holidays in the open air (a developer of previously unsuspected muscles) is the archaeological training dig.

Intellectual or *cognitive development*, if not a more important field than physical development, is certainly one to which history must be more directly pertinent, and is currently an area of great interest to educationists. It can be subdivided into categories of increasing generality. Historical material may be used in the training of *skills*: in the infant and lower junior school, in reading, writing, number, painting and modelling; in the middle school, in the development of extended writing, in dialogue and plays, in calculation, measuring and planning; and in secondary schools, in more sophisticated skills like costume-making, photography and film-making. History contributes to *conceptual development* in raising problems of distance, space and scale, but most important, in the development of the cluster of concepts about time, from an understanding of centuries, millennia and generations, to an appreciation of the complex series of events which constitute a single day. It serves as an introduction to the nature of *evidence*, to varied kinds of evidence and their interrelationship, to impartial assessment and elementary research procedures; and an increasing amount of material using first-hand evidence is now available for schools (Fines, 1968, p. 548). History provides generous scope for *analysis*, for the making of logical distinctions, the awareness of separate issues, the marshalling of points and the construction of arguments; the ordering of events, the description of stages and causes and effects, is a necessary if sometimes over-emphasized part of a historical training. And a case has already been made out in Chapter 2 for history as a mode of developing higher cognitive skills under the general name of *judgment*; the ability to use one's own judgment and diverge from received ideas, to tolerate uncertainty and ambiguity, to illustrate by analogy and metaphor, to harness imagery and fantasy in rational processes.

Emotional or *affective* development contributes to the

character and personality of the child, rather than to this thinking ability. Here, history must be seen in its relationship to expressive activities like art and music, to poetry, drama and the novel, and in another direction, to religion. All these subjects make distinctive contributions to the child's personal development. But it seems to me that history has a particular contribution, because by definition it seeks to be about reality, about people who really were and events which really happened, but yet about a reality which does not involve the tension and pain of the present. The power of literature and the arts over the imagination is moderated by the ultimate realization that they are fiction; we can say if we wish that *Macbeth* is grand but impossible. The power of history is moderated rather differently by the knowledge that it is not happening now, it is not happening to us, though it is indeed possible. History thus provides a special kind of vicarious experience (Fines, 1969, pp. vi-vii; Bruner, 1960, p. 81).

The impact of this experience on the growing child has several interrelated effects: in an increasingly objective self-concept, in an acceptance of change, in adjustment to reality and in the taking of roles. One of the most important concepts in Piaget's thinking is egocentricity and its reverse, the state of equilibrium. Piaget places great stress on the importance for a child's general conceptual development of passing out of stages of egocentric behaviour in early childhood and again in adolescence. Social psychologists call this process 'ego-development' (Sherif and Sherif, 1956, pp. 594-8). Direct experience, both with objects and with other people, is of course important in persuading the child that a real world exists outside of and independent of himself. But indirect experience in books and culture is also important, and indeed has some advantages. Through history the child comes to grasp that he is just one of countless human beings who have led autonomous lives—and because they are in the past, he cannot go about actively proving to them his own self-importance, as he might do in direct experience. In one sense, history is a highly subjective subject; but in another sense it is more objective than our present experience. We come to realize that Pepys, Boswell and Celia Fiennes will remain splendidly themselves even when our present generation has passed away. And as a result of such a realization, we have to look at ourselves more objectively.

Second, we come to understand and accept the nature of change in time, with the implications this has for the conduct of our own lives. We see that our own attitudes, indeed our settled opinions, can change, perhaps suddenly, more often imperceptibly. So too do the attitudes of people we know, sometimes converging and sometimes diverging from our own. The nature of society is also constantly changing, both absolutely and in its relationship to ourselves. And within this change we must recognize the play of the contingent and the unpredictable. The lives of men like Henry VIII or Charles II or Neville Chamberlain provide extended examples of the fluctuating sympathies both of individuals and of masses of people.

Third, history, like other disciplines which seek to give accounts of human behaviour, enables us to anticipate, to think through and accept, aspects of the human condition which might otherwise be unexpected and disturbing. This is true both of the more sombre aspects—ill-luck, disappointment, failure, tragedy, cruelty, sickness, ageing and death—and of more neutral aspects—the ups-and-downs of life, the oddities of human behaviour and the unexpected qualities of people. Looked at more positively, a historical awareness may help us to anticipate events and cope with them more easily, to face them with equanimity and good humour. Such development, seen as an educational objective, is in the 'generalized set' category of Bloom's affective domain (Krathwohl, et al., 1964).

No one would wish to claim that such awareness provides any kind of anodyne for the human condition: but it would be difficult to deny history's contribution to raising the level of our response to life above that of the primitive and the savage (Bruner, 1966, p. 101). History gives this experience in a great variety of forms: in biography, say of Eduard Benes or Napoleon III or Mary Tudor, in a slice of history, like the reaction of Britain to the threatened invasion of 1940, or in an extended topic such as disease and public health in the nineteenth century. And this is an aspect of history in which local studies and quite modest research can be as effective as better known themes: an interview with an elderly person, a survey of gravestones and memorial tablets in a church, a few pages of a parish register, the archives of a workhouse and the records of a charitable trust—these may provide a more searching introduction to both pure and applied history than a conventionally studied 'period'.

Another aspect of the child's development is role-taking, the learning of social roles. Role theory and the theory of reference groups are important themes in modern sociology (Sherif and Sherif, 1969, p. 418 sq.). Young people in particular clearly identify reference groups or reference sets—model girls, the heroes of Westerns, pop groups, Georgie Best—on which they attempt to model their appearance, behaviour and attitudes. Day-dreaming and the vicarious acting-out of roles then enable young people progressively to evolve modes of behaviour suitable to their own personalities. And although the expectations of the individuals and social groups which a young person actually meets—parents, peer group, factory mates—are very important in determining the roles he adopts, vicarious experience is almost as influential. Perhaps the most significant function of popular culture is the provision of reference figures, but the more formal culture of religion, drama, the novel, geography and history also plays its part. Indeed, all subjects provide these opportunities; the young scientist and engineer are not just *doing* science and engineering, they are *being* scientists and engineers. And the importance in the learning of roles of transmitted culture, in comparison with direct experience, is that culture, by presenting a vast canvas of possible kinds of behaviour, is much more likely than experience to be an agency of social change. An example of such change is the gradual breaking-away of Protestant individuals and families from close-knit peasant communities in the early modern period, characteristically effected by the reading of the Bible and the discovery in it of powerful and novel role conceptions.

In contemporary English society, the selective educational system has a two-way relationship to this process. Children who have sometimes accidentally acquired dynamic role-conceptions through reading, thereafter thrust their way into the system, and once they are in it, the system provides them with increasingly diverse reference categories. Put simply, at a critical point, some children cease to accept that they are going to be mechanics and shop assistants in local society, and come to believe that they are going to be generals and surgeons like the ones they read about; fifteen years later they have in fact become college lecturers and social workers. It is precisely in this way that 'advantaged' and 'disadvantaged' children are distinguished, by the presence or absence of a dynamic role-conception. And I would suggest that the frequent failure of 'secondary modern' forms of education lies in their inability to transmit such conceptions to children, which is an argument for the more effective teaching of history and literary subjects to 'Newsom' children.

Infants and juniors

In the phrase 'Once upon a time', the affective function of

history has common origins with literature; when we have
uttered those magic words the child can safely experience
the thrilling and sometimes painful events that follow.
That is why we do indeed start learning history as infants,
and not even in the infant school, but in the pre-school
story; we start learning it by developing a balanced and
alert response to stories. Thereafter, it is not difficult to
begin touching on historical aspects of the material. *Peter
Rabbit* and *Jemima Puddleduck* are exciting stories, but
they are not just the world of 'Once upon a time'. If we
look at their illustrations in particular, we can see that
they are in another time, a time which we may establish
as when grandfather was a little boy. And not long after,
we shall be reading aloud from *The Borrowers*, set firmly
in a well-realized past, then *The Railway Children*, written
out of the past itself (Plowden Report, 1967, p. 620 sq.).

We can see the next stage as the children's establishment of a *self-concept*, a recognition that they *are* children
with a role in social life, with expected modes of behaviour
and a distinctive relationship with adults. They progress
gradually from identifying first with animal-children—
Peter Rabbit, Winnie the Pooh, Larry the Lamb; then with
imaginary children in stories—Millie-Mollie-Mandy, Alice,
Just William; afterwards with imaginary children in history like those of *The Wool-Pack* or the *People of the Past*
series; and thence with real children in the past, young
James Cook, young James Watt, or young Napoleon. All
the time, the stories are acting as mirrors against which
the child rehearses and plays out concepts of what he is
and what he ought to be, raising questions and suggesting
answers, about relationships with people, and personal
bearing, about conduct and morality.

We can recognize too in these early stories the function
of the *father-figure*, as a hero, an exemplar and the pro-
vider of security. Arthur, Richard I, Nelson and many
other historical characters, graphically portrayed for in-

stance by Ladybird books, play this important role. And as we shall see later, they help the child particularly about age 6-7, to begin to think through the problem of danger and death for this revered figure.

When they are a little older, at 7-8, children move into a 'them-and-us' phase of gangs, cowboys and Indians, cops and robbers. Historical material lends itself well to this phase, being essentially concerned, as we have seen, with debate, with showing two sides of a question. This is the time for Greeks and Trojans, Romans and Carthaginians, Puritans and Cavaliers, and so on.

Soon, too, children become concerned with a conception of their *sex-roles* (Gabriel, 1968, p. 278). A girl grows to be less of a tomboy and more of a little woman. It is time for stories about girls as well as about heroes, for queens and princesses, for Helen, Cleopatra, Boudicca, Joan of Arc, and Elizabeth, and a little later for Elizabeth Fry, Florence Nightingale and Marie Curie. This is in fact one of the areas in which normally inexhaustible historical material is rather thin. Women have not had a good press in history, and the range of stories about women, suitable for any particular age-range and which provide the teacher with sufficient material, is quite limited. To compensate, the teacher has to make full use of literary sources and historical novels in which girls share the adventures with boys—for example, the novels of E. Nesbit.

By 8-9 many children are passing through the final stages of forming a concept of death (Anthony, 1940). This process has been going on since 4—perhaps the most important point about Peter Rabbit and Jemima Puddleduck is that we all know (though we hardly dare say) what will happen to them if they don't escape, and many of the best-known fairy stories—'The Sleeping Beauty', 'Snow White', 'The Tin Soldier'—are about death and mortal danger. *The Water Babies* and 'The Little Match Girl' are examples of affecting stories which in this respect close the gap between fairy stories and history. Then history itself is full of stories which serve to adjust and reconcile children to the notion of death and dying—the Spartans at Thermopylae, Robin Hood, Charles I, Nelson, Livingstone and so on. In this way, in showing children the most difficult piece of human knowledge held at arm's length by being in the past, history performs its most important 'applied' function.

As children move through the middle school and become aware of physical growth and of the passing of time, they become more involved in the process of growing-up, in becoming less like children, and they are interested in stories which show this process. *The Children of the New Forest* has already been noticed; the Victorian novels of G. A. Henty are also skilful at transforming athletic boys at the beginning of the story into much-decorated heroes— and married men—at the end. Stories of growing-up, particularly from a difficult or humble youth to applauded maturity, are popular at this stage: Henry V is a familiar example of wild youth turned hero, and for girls the accessions of Elizabeth and of Victoria may have a quality of magic.

The secondary school

Until puberty, most normal children have an uninhibited interest in history. But after puberty the position changes: a minority go on reading historical novels (Jeffrey Farnol or Hugh Walpole perhaps) and making detailed studies of nineteenth-century railways, but a majority lose interest and may in fact become positively hostile. It is difficult of course to distinguish this loss of interest from the circumstances in which it arises; bad history taught badly over several years may have produced its own reward. But there are obviously some general factors involved. The children are moving into what Gesell calls 'the 15-year-old slump' with its 'hostile attitude' (1956, pp. 219, 241). They become critical of the adult world as represented by their parents, teachers and 'the authorities' and, of course, most of history is about 'the authorities'; it is about adults, who are now regarded not as glamorous figures for reference and identification, but as blundering bores (it is worth noting that although 'Children in History' is a well-developed theme, 'Adolescents in History' is not). But as well as rejecting adults, they also want to reject the children they once were, and to put away childish things. As I have noted elsewhere, this is the age when dusty collections of stamps, flints and pottery are lost in the backs of cupboards (1969, p. 75). And history as they have learned it in the junior and middle school *is* a childish thing; the very enthusiasm which they gave to it, the friezes, the dressing-up, the pageants, now come to seem merely shaming.

Let us look at some figures for this loss of interest. Wall's now ageing survey of the educational preferences of adolescents, in categories of 'disliked' and 'disliked very much', showed modern history as the fifth most disliked of twenty-eight subjects; in a rating of increases of interest since age 15, 'lives of great men and women' evinced least interest, followed by poetry, then by history (Wall, 1948, pp. 102, 122-5). In a more recent survey, 41 per cent of the boys and 40 per cent of the girls gave history an 'interest' rating, only 29 per cent of all children gave it a 'usefulness' rating, and 28-29 per cent of parents an 'importance' rating (Schools Council, 1968).

How are we to deal with this apparently unavoidable problem in the secondary school? One answer is to stop teaching history for several years, but it is an important reservation that it must be administratively easy for children to take up history later without being damned for ever for not having attempted CSE or 'O' level examinations. Another solution may be to make history for several years an optional subject (Newsom Report, 1963, para. 531), preferably not as a simple either/or with geography, but as part of a package of options. Again, it is essential that children should not be penalized for dropping this subject, but should have every opportunity of returning to it. We would not in any case expect that the history they would 'miss' at 14 or 15 would be part of a methodical syllabus leading up to 'O' or 'A' levels (see Chapter 5).

But if it should be argued that a thread of continuity in history should be maintained throughout the secondary school, a number of measures can still be taken. We could, first, reduce the amount of time devoted to the subject so that it should not seem too obtrusive or oppressive. Second, we can select topics which are novel and which represent a break with 'childish' history. Third, we can choose historical topics related to those interests which children *do* have in the secondary school (and the surveys show what these are). Fourth, we can try to teach what history we do keep very much better, and this will normally require a greater readiness by the school and by education authorities to spend the kind of money on historical equipment and visits which they are probably already spending on science laboratories, craft workshops and geography rooms (Newsom Report, para. 506). If history is worth attempting at all in the secondary school, it is worth doing as well as we can do it.

Table 1 indicates an approach to the first and second points above. It shows a contraction of history teaching to only seven topics at 14+, including single, carefully selected topics from pre-history, local history and British history, and with an emphasis on relatively unfamiliar topics from European, American and world history.

In choosing secondary school topics we should look for opportunities of integrating the historical topics with themes and subjects in which the children are likely to

75

Table 1 Possible components of a continuous history curriculum for British schools

Age	Projects or topics covered
5+	1
6+	1 4 4 4
7+	1 3 4 4 4 4 4 5
8+	1 2 3 4 4 4 4 4 4 5 5
9+	1 2 3 3 4 4 4 4 4 4 5 5 5 6
10+	1 2 2 3 3 3 3 4 4 4 4 4 4 5 5 5 6 6
11+	1 2 3 3 3 4 4 4 4 5 5 6 6 7
12+	1 2 3 3 4 4 4 5 5 6 6 7
13+	2 3 4 4 5 5 6 7
14+	2 3 4 5 5 6 7
15+	2 3 3 4 4 5 5 5 6 7
16+	2 2 3 3 4 4 4 5 5 5 6 6 7
17+	2 2 3 3 3 4 4 4 5 5 5 5 6 6 6 7 7
% of total timetable	2% 3% 4%

Key: 1 = World stories, e.g. Trojan Horse, Arabian Nights, Robin Hood (total—8 topics)
2 = Prehistory, including archaeology and anthropology (total—13 topics)
3 = Local history and field-work (22 topics)
4 = English and British history (44 topics)
5 = European, colonial and North American history (27 topics)
6 = World history associated with Europe, e.g. Mohammedan conquests, Boxer rising (15 topics)
7 = World history autonomous of Europe, e.g. ancient China, India, Africa and South America before the Europeans (8 topics)

be interested. We know, for instance, that they are interested in themselves, in their own personalities and problems. As we have seen, their adulation of sportsmen and reading of women's magazines make it clear that, like younger children, they need to identify with other people; but adolescents expect their identification/ reference figures to be much closer to what they see as reality than do younger children. A characteristic way in which such identification figures are translated into the language of the adolescent is in their interpretation by an acceptable modern personality on film, television or the stage; by Kirk Douglas as Ulysses, or Elizabeth Taylor as Cleopatra, or Richard Burton as Henry VIII. Film then is one way in which we can establish contact with the preoccupations of adolescents, and having done so, we can move away from the more specifically to the less specifically personal, to *Glencoe* and *Culloden*, or to the film *The Red Badge of Courage*, or by using film strip, slides or radio-vision, to undramatized personal stories like those of the Duke of Windsor or President Kennedy (Schools Council/Nuffield, 1970, p. 14).

A second and very obvious area of interest of adolescents has already been noticed—the other sex, romance and love. This is of course, as many teachers of biology and religious studies and visiting speakers on marriage guidance will know, an area full of dangers. But the subject is, in my view, a nettle which secondary school history teachers must at some point grasp. The children are in any case going to giggle and write rude verses about Henry VIII, George IV, and the many other inviting topics, and it is better that love and passion should be treated as important components of historical character and situation than that they should be laboriously avoided. Victorian and Edwardian morality and the rise of the 'permissive society', for instance, is a complex historical theme, involving not only sexual morality, but attitudes to women, drink, drugs, crime, religious practice and artistic values. All kinds of individuals, from George Eliot to Oscar Wilde and D. H. Lawrence, make their appearance. Similar historical themes are offered by the moral character of the Restoration or of Hogarth's London or

77

of the Regency period, all of which provide good literary and artistic material and give opportunities for discussing the place of religion in society. Over the whole modern period, morality and family life can be discussed in relation to population growth and family limitation, and for an earlier period may be considered as part of an anthropological approach to past customs and traditions. 'Relations between the sexes' is one of the topics of the Schools Council/Nuffield Humanities Project (ibid., p. 6).

As Gesell observed a generation ago, young people are readily involved with current affairs, world problems and world conditions (Gesell *et al.*, 1956, pp. 243, 342), with the bomb, the environment, poverty, colour prejudice and so on. This suggests that we should select contemporary themes with a strong historical background: war and weaponry, the Second World War and Hiroshima, gas in the First World War, guns and nineteenth-century colonization, the brutal reality of eigthteenth-century naval warfare; perhaps environmental problems in the nineteenth century, waste disposal, sewerage, water supply, adulteration of food and housing (Newsom Report, para. 511). In general, either recent historical events—the First World War, the thirties, the Second World War—or remote, strange places like Japan or Peru, may offer more attractive topics than the familiar historical stories. At the same time, the mode of treatment should range from the factual and practical, as in studies of the mechanisms of firearms or of methods of making garments, to the generalized and discursive, in discussions of racialism, crime and punishment, Women's Lib., or even of possible cyclical movements in history (Gesell *et al.*, 1956, p. 243). The methodical middle way of the causes of the French Revolution may not be appropriate to this age range.

The need of adolescents for physical activity can be usefully combined with a practical approach to history in well-planned and precisely limited field-work projects, in assistance with archaeological excavations and in industrial archaeology. These can be followed up in the school by the design and construction of substantial, even full-scale working models—scissors-and-paste and cardboard models are less successful with this age-range. In another direction, industrial archaeology can be followed up in the history of firms and industries, and of commercial activity. Again, what is required is not a bland, whitewashing 'official' history, but a history in which deficiencies, mistakes and disputes are thoroughly explored. Moreover, the story should not be tailed off in the Edwardian period, but brought systematically forward into the working environment which the children will experience.

Adolescent children read a good deal, though the material, well-thumbed papers, magazines and paperbacks which are passed around the class, is often of a very low standard (Gabriel, 1968, p. 509). English normally has a higher score in surveys than history, and 'Books and Reading' had a surprisingly high sixth place in Wall's list of increases in interest (Schools Council, 1968; Wall, 1948). As many talented teachers have shown, these literary interests can be both deepened and employed with historical material in integrated topics: John Steinbeck and inter-war America, for instance, George Orwell and inter-war Britain, Robert Graves and the First World War, D. H. Lawrence and industrial society. This is another area in which the children's interest in the mass media can be harnessed with the use of good audio-visual aids, film, radio and records. Films like *The Grapes of Wrath*, *Of Mice and Men*, and *For Whom The Bell Tolls* offer powerful and compelling introductions to the historical aspects of their subjects (Newsom Report, paras 474-6; Schools Council/ Nuffield, 1970, p. 14).

We have noted that adolescent children are hostile to and critical of adults—their parents and teachers, adults in the street, the adult generation—and that the heroes and saints of the junior school later become prigs and stuffed shirts fit only for parody and ridicule. But this mood also gives the children an interest in the mistakes of the past, in blunders and stupidities, in the clay feet of heroes; they want to know that adults make mistakes. 'Unnecessary' wars like the Crimea, the Boer War, the First and Second World Wars, Suez and Vietnam provide useful material here. And we ought to take a Lytton-Stracheyish look at some of the heroes, and ask whether Cromwell was a brutal hypocrite, Bonnie Prince Charlie an ass, or Lord Shaftesbury a bigoted reactionary.

No one who has handled children of this age will suppose that the suggestions of the last few pages will solve many of the problems of teaching them history. And we can recall that we began the discussion by suggesting that there were indeed some advantages in not teaching history at this age; or that it might be offered only to those children who have chosen it, not as a soft option, but because they have preferred it in a list of attractive alternatives. But if we do have to teach history between 13 and 15, then, provided we do not attempt too much—perhaps half-a-dozen topics each year—we can choose these topics from a number of areas in which there is a good chance of arousing and maintaining interest, and of achieving, not the methodical coverage of 'periods', but the broadening of historical sympathies.

Young adults

But age 15 is the nadir of interest in history. With the growing maturity of 16, and the signs of slowly returning sympathy with adults noted by Gesell, comes a developing historical sense (Gabriel, 1968, p. 355). The ratings of Young School Leavers suggest a quite striking growth both in interest and a sense of utility with increasing age; parents too think that history is more important as their children get older. By 16 over half the children will probably think history is interesting, and by 17 to 18, up to 70 per cent of them are likely to think it interesting and about half to think it is useful. This evidence can then be linked with what we know of the subjects chosen at sixth form, college and university levels, with the popularity of history as a subject in adult education, and with our discussion of history as part of popular culture. This is one of the fields in which the raising of the school-leaving age, and the increasing numbers staying on beyond, raise, not a nightmare of yet more hideous problems, but a prospect of a breakthrough to a better response. An attenuation of history courses in the middle school, followed by a vigorous modernized history course in the leaving year can be seen to be an appropriate strategy for the secondary school curriculum. The last of history's applied functions in the school is now taking place—the appreciation of the nature of adult reality, the completion of an understanding of the passage of time, the adjustment to death and suffering, an understanding of failure, a tolerance of uncertainty, a recognition of chance. Here, applied history comes close to pure history; in helping the adolescent to learn in these ways, it is introducing him to the texture of history itself.

5

Aspects of curriculum and method

In the previous chapters I have attempted to analyse what we mean by history and what are the characteristic features which follow from that definition; I have offered an account of the psychology of learning history, and have tried to show how history thus interpreted can contribute to children's development. We are now in a position to make suggestions for a school history curriculum and for teaching methods which bring together these various themes and are consistent with them.

We can begin generally by saying that school history should be of such a kind and taught in such a manner as to evoke a historical response, and to develop a sense of the past; that this objective should have priority over the teaching of knowledge, or chronological coverage, or the inculcation of technical skills. It does not follow of course that the kind of history which evokes a response will necessarily be colourful or romantic. It does mean that we shall be looking for material capable of engrossing pupils of the age-range we are concerned with; we shall want to secure in the pupils a sense of personal involvement and an on-going intellectual commitment to the study of the material. But we should certainly not have a puritanical distaste for colour and romance. From a psychological point of view, we want to give the child a series of memorable images capable of recall in concrete form, which can be subconsciously linked with other images and mulled over in reverie and day-dream. The child then has to have time to ruminate over this material, and afterwards needs opportunities to bring the material out, barnacle-encrusted, in his own original and perhaps divergent account of the events.

We can suggest that children should be encouraged to range widely over historical material, experiencing its breadth and variety, and having the opportunity to find analogies between different bits of the material. At the same time, a child should encounter a limited number of topics frequently enough for him to experience the deepening process, the search for greater validity, characteristic of the subject. Children can be made aware that historical narrative is dependent on evidence, and introduced to various kinds of evidence. But they must also be helped to see that the evidence has its limitations, that historical statements are matters of greater or less probability and that there are disagreements about the conclusions we draw.

We can expect that a historical curriculum will include studies of individual people, and of their youth, maturation, ageing and death. It should deal with what I have called generational time, the relationship of human beings to the passage of years and decades, the subtle pattern of change within individuals, families and generations and the transmission and modification of culture in societies. It may involve the study of individuals in groups, both small groups of families, confidantes and friends, and larger groups of communities and nations. Opportunities can be given for children to identify with people in the past, and at the same time to experience the great variety of forms of human behaviour. While remaining firmly rooted in the concrete, a curriculum can introduce more analytic and abstract modes of interpretation, and though at no stage omitting the elementary historical situations—individual achievements, the clash of 'right' and 'wrong', the duel of personalities—it will progressively develop the study of more complex situations in which a number of equally valued individuals can be seen interacting within shifting social patterns. Failure needs to be studied as well as success, the 'what might have been' as well as the 'what actually transpired'.

A discontinuous curriculum

A characteristic fault of historical curricula is that they try to cover too much material; and a good deal of this material consists of what Bruner calls the 'middle language', between the concrete illustration and the illuminating general concept (Bruner, 1960, p. 14). In Namier's words, 'what matters in history is the great outline and the significant detail: what must be avoided is the deadly morass of irrelevant narrative' (1956, p. 379). In considering a history curriculum, we can begin then by discarding the supposition that it has to be continuous, progressive and increasingly specialized over the whole span of school life. There is in fact no objective evidence to support this familiar scheme. For many years, children have begun new subjects, like languages, at age 11, economics at 16, or law at 18, and then pursued them to advance academic levels. Many adult learners, for instance in the Open University, have been able to take up new subject learning successfully. And on the other hand, children already drop subjects—dance, drama, art, music—throughout their educational careers, though it is reasonably assumed that what they have done in those areas will be of benefit to them for long afterwards.

There is much to be gained from interrupting a particular mode of study for a time, to prevent boredom and rekindle the pleasure of novelty on return to it; adult learners often come back to refresher courses with renewed zest and interest. And we should not suppose that during the intervals when we are not teaching a subject formally at school the child is not learning anything; this is particularly true of history. It may be that the informal learning of film, television and magazines has an important role in improving motivation at the next stage in formal learning. Much research needs to be done on the advantages and disadvantages of discontinuous learning, but at least it would be safe to predict that when we have the results of such research, it will show that the optimum conditions vary widely from subject to subject.

Another assumption we can question is that the best preparation for work in a particular subject is always work at a lower level in the same subject. There are in fact discontinuities in the learning of different subjects. About 13, for instance, when the child has done a good deal of work on standard British history, there may be no point in moving him on to similar work in standard European history. An actual move forward in history may require a conceptual jump (perhaps of a Piagetian kind) for which he is not ready. But at the same time, the child may in geography be developing a particular kind of elementary analytical skill which will transfer readily to the less precise historical material later on, and for a time, it may be to his long-term advantage in history to spend his time doing geography. Literature and history may have a similar relationship at 17. And there is a time-honoured relationship about 20 between the learning of Latin and Greek, ancient history and philosophy.

With these considerations in mind we can look critically at primary school curricula which begin with the Egyptians, Greeks and Romans at 7, go on to the Anglo-Saxons, Normans and the Middle Ages at 8, to Tudors and Stuarts at 9, and reach Hanoverians and Victoria at 10; and at secondary curricula which methodically recapitulate the story with the addition of European topics; ancient history at 11, medieval history at 12, Renaissance, Reformation and Wars of Religion at 13, Wars of English Succession, Spanish Succession, Austrian Succession, Seven Years' War and American Revolution at 14, thus leaving the French Revolution and the nineteenth century as the hallowed stamping ground of 'O' level. We can consider instead possible curricula which are discontinuous internally, being made up of a series of projects or topics linked together only in a spiral pattern (see p. 49), or discontinuous over the school life, either as in Table 1 by a fluctuating pattern of time allocated, or by leaving breaks of one or more years in which no history is taught.

As an alternative to Table 1, history teaching might be arranged in a series of blocks, each of which could aim at different objectives, select different material and use different techniques. One arguable pattern of such blocks and breaks might be for instance: age 6-8, a history story-telling book; 8-10, a break, filled perhaps by environmental studies or social studies; 10-13, a standard British history block; 13-16, a break, filled perhaps by geography, by introductory sociology and psychology or work similar to the Schools Council/Nuffield Humanities Project; 16-19, a broad foundation-course history block; 19-21, a break, occupied perhaps with economics and statistics; 21-24, a historical research block; with political history and cultural history blocks available as refresher courses and in adult education.

Chronology

The debate over children's understanding of a chronological scheme for history well illustrates a point made in Chapter 1. We suppose that children have no understanding while adults have a good understanding of chronology. But it is more accurate to say that children have a crude understanding of chronology and normal adults a better but still imperfect understanding of it. Even professional historians, in phrases like 'the sudden collapse of medieval society', 'a speedy return to normality in the decade after 1815', or 'the events leading to the Second World War followed in rapid succession', sometimes reveal an inadequate understanding of the passage of time.

Our definition of history as a response to a past event suggests that children do not need to know a chronological scheme in order to experience history; they only need to conceive of an event as having occurred in the past. Between 4 and 6, children can distinguish 'Once upon a time' as the first category into which such events can be put, a category which makes it possible for fear, pain, death, loss of parents to be contemplated without real danger of involvement. But 'Once upon a time', though an essential preliminary, cannot, with its talking animals, fantasy and magic, be considered a historical concept. It is from about 6 that normal children make a firm distinction between the Julius Caesars and William the Conquerors of 'Once upon a time' stories, and the Winnie-the-Poohs and Rupert Bears who inhabit the same territory. At 6 many children know that Nelson was a real person who died, and whose death occurred before the memory of anyone now alive. The important further step, of grasping that in a hundred years' time *we* shall all be dead and be people in history, is not long in following. I have a tape-recording of a six-year-old explaining just this point to me. Robin Hood and Captain Cook now exist as historical individuals, and 'cavemen', 'the Romans' and 'knights' as historic groups. Whether they existed all at the same time or in some sequence is not at first clear. But a frontrunner soon appears in the shape of 'Stone-age Kit, the Ancient Brit' in the comics, or *Stig of the Dump* and *The Cave*

87

Twins in the reading books: to wit, Stone-Age Man. He is obviously first because he wears least clothes and uses stones as tools; if asked, the children may tell you that he came 'just after Adam and Eve'.

By 7, most children have a three-stage chronological framework: the Stone Age, history, and nowadays (their memory span). Within history, Ulysses, Richard the Lionheart and Robert Stephenson exist as parts of memorable episodes without sequential connection. But broad groups of characteristics are gradually brought together, so that by 9, the framework typically has five stages: the Stone Age, the Greeks and Romans, 'medieval', Tudors to Victoria, and recent history (what grandad did in the War). Thereafter, between 10 and 13, there is a progressive distinction of sub-stages: Republican Rome, for instance, is recognized as earlier than Imperial Rome, the Normans are seen as an earlier stage of the Middle Ages than the Wars of the Roses, the Stuarts are fitted in between Elizabeth and the Georges.

By 13, most children have the kind of chronological framework that they will retain as average adults, one which enables historical material to be well enough sorted and identified for its stories to be enjoyed without discomfort, but which is very generalized and which has awkward gaps. Take the ancient Egyptians, for example—they are well realized as a concept, but where do they come in the sequence? Or the Anglo-Saxons—do they come, as I have been asked, before or after the Romans? And what about that odd gap between Bonnie Prince Charlie (who nicely ends the Stuarts) and James Watt (with whom the Industrial Revolution is often begun)?— sometimes, even for eighteen-year-old students, the whole eighteenth century seems to slip through it. And of course the process is never complete. We all set up a chronological framework to accommodate that material with which we are familiar, but remain in a child-like state with the rest.

How many professional historians, asked whether Ming came before Tang, Theodoric before Justinian, Charles IX before Francis II, Rockingham before Shelburne and Cleveland before Garfield, would score five out of five?

This conception of the way children learn a chronology conforms with the way we think as adults, about our own lives, about contemporary affairs and about history. We think about episodes in a rough framework, and only if necessary fill in a precise, dated framework between them. If we are asked, at very short notice, to give a talk on the history of our own times, a series of episodes will come by association into the mind—Ireland, Vietnam, Kennedy, Cuba, CND, Gaitskell, Suez, and so on; we may then make a few lines of notes on each, and arrange them in a framework which will not necessarily be chronological. Similarly, asked to write a script for a pageant of the village's history, I might start with Charles I's arrest, Henry VI's marriage, the supposed association with Shakespeare, the medieval monks; and on consideration, I might decide that the story would be better told backwards rather than forwards.

We can conclude, then, first, that all schoolchildren are capable of learning history, in the sense that they have some notion of a pattern of real events in past time into which new material can be fitted. But, second, that because this pattern is so generalized and imprecise, there is no point in the teacher organizing his work on a detailed chronological basis (which, if he is honest, he himself may only recall with the aid of notes). Indeed, there is a positive argument against step-by-step chronology: that initially children are *more* capable of grasping the notion of change in time if successive topics are so differentiated by dress, weapons, mode of transport and so on as to be memorable. William and Mary to Anne may really be just 'one damn thing after another': but between the Eliza-

bethan theatre and the Victorian music hall, times had un-
mistakably changed.

It is better to use some other principle of organization
than temporal sequence—perhaps thematic, perhaps
merely one of novelty and variety—and to allow various
linking themes to collect the chronological framework
together in the course of a block of study. A psychologic-
ally sound way, then, of making up a history curriculum,
is to arrange episodes or topics in a sequence based sometimes on chronology but often on some other principle,
interrupted from time to time by a project more specifically chronological which unobtrusively strings many of
the episodes together: a frieze perhaps, a study of costume
down the ages, a family tree, a time-line, or a quiz on
dates (which is popular if not attempted too often).

Stereotypes

This notion of a chronological framework as a series of
episodes slowly linked together over the school life takes
us back to a consideration of the nature of historical concepts, and to some general points about conceptualization
in children. Some implications of Vygotsky's analysis of
children's learning in terms of 'pseudo-concepts' and
'proto-concepts' have been discussed in Chapter 2 (and see
Watts, 1969, pp. 55-6). Children learn (and we attempt to
teach), not by putting together lots of little bits of correct
information, but by forming a large vague impression of
a subject, and then making it more precise and refined. This
is how, I have argued, we develop a concept of 'the past'.
It is also how, for instance, a beginning student of education
first encounters and conceives of a subject like educational
psychology. For new learners, the large vague impression
of a new concept may be little better than a day-dream
or nightmare. But the impression is quickly turned into a
crude and more manageable concept by the identification

of one or two memorable characteristics. Take for example the old Services tag for a psychiatrist—a 'trick cyclist' : this is a play on words, a witty metaphor, a visual image, an easier phrase to speak and spell; it enabled men to give some kind of identity to a person whose role would otherwise have been vague and threatening, and helped them, as it were, to put him in his place.

The crude impression then is a caricature, a symbol in itself, or a small collection of symbols, which make the concept instantly recognizable, the stereotype of Chapter 2. We all know the stereotypes in children's art—the face with two eyes, a nose and a mouth, the body with four limbs and a head, the house with four windows, a door and a chimney. Learning, at least in part, consists of refining stereotypes. At what point we pass from refining stereotypes to learning about the 'real' thing is a very difficult question, particularly in history; one could argue that even at an advanced level, Hobsbawm and Hartwell for instance are still struggling with stereotypes of the Industrial Revolution, and Trevor-Roper, Stone and others with stereotypes of 'the gentry'. We can say that because we cannot cope with all knowledge, we simplify much of it, and enable it to be more easily memorized and recalled by turning it into stereotypes. And we are concerned here with children : for them, 'history' itself is a stereotype, which as teachers we progressively refine from its beginning as a comic strip to a modest level of subtlety.

The 'facts' of history too are stereotypes. When, for example, I asked a seven-year-old to tell me something about the Romans he said that they were 'fighters' : there is the stereotype—a thousand years of civilization reduced to a single word easily comprehended by a small boy. But not, however, an entirely misleading notion : 'war' would be a plausible theme by which to analyse Roman history. The boy could of course also draw the stereotype; it would be a man in a short skirt and round helmet, carrying a rectangular shield and a spear and wearing shin-guards. We have already met the stereotype 'Stone-Age man'. He wears a skin over one shoulder, has matted hair, and carries a large club with an unhistorical nail in it. And we all know the stereotype 'Viking'. He is bearded, wears a conical helmet with wings or horns and travels in boats with round shields on the sides and striped sails. So too the stereotype 'Norman', who wears chain mail, and has a conical helmet with a piece on the front which comes over his nose and presses it down. He is easily linked with the stereotype 'battle of Hastings' (two groups of fighters, and one man with an arrow in his eye). That quite difficult period for children, the eighteenth century, can be usefully approached through three stereotypes—pirates, smugglers and highwaymen. Then there are 'Crusaders', 'Roundheads', 'Victorians' and dozens or others. We can see stereotypes used in an adult context, for example, on the covers of the Open University Foundation course units.

Some commentators on children's learning of history have been shocked to discover that children think in stereotypes, that their stereotypes are so crude, and have concluded that this makes it difficult if not impossible to teach history to them (Peel, 1967, pp. 169-70). Quite the reverse is true; stereotypes are distinctive, colourful memory aids to children, and are the cues to stored associations. You would not set a ten-year-old child a question: 'Discuss the events of the year 1745.' You would ask him about 'Bonnie Prince Charlie', and a flood of associations would pour out. Within five minutes, with a little prompting, you might have some account of the '45 and Culloden, some impressions of eighteenth-century warfare, quite sensible views on the Stuart and Hanoverian dynasties and some opinions on the history of Scotland. You might then add the new and interesting bit of information, that James Wolfe was at Culloden, which gives a relationship between two sets of stereotypes and establishes a chronological sequence.

And if the rest of the class has been as interested as the original respondent, they will then be ready for some research of their own, some art, music or drama, maps of the St Lawrence and the like.

The crudeness of the stereotype is irrelevant to the fact that it provides the lively starting point for genuine historical exploration. Within ten minutes of talking about the battle of Hastings, the class might be looking at pictures of the Bayeux Tapestry, at a duplicated passage from the Anglo-Saxon Chronicle and at photocopies of facsimile pages of Domesday Book; within twenty minutes they could be standing under the Norman doorway at the church. Introduce the stereotype of the Victorian in his stove-pipe hat, and soon you can be showing slides of Victorian photographs and discussing changing women's fashions from 1870 to the present day—one effective way of tying together 'history' and 'nowadays'. It would be fatal however to deaden the stereotype by over-exposure and over-teaching. Don't try to ensure that the children have learned everything about the subject; this is an impossible aim. Your aim is to give them a historical experience, and to leave them a little better equipped to deepen it the next time they encounter the topic.

This is one purpose of the spiral curriculum. Children will encounter historical topics several times in their school life. Bonnie Prince Charlie and Flora Macdonald will appear as stereotypes at 8, and the children sing some songs; at 12, the children can experience something of the horror of Culloden and the brutality of the pacification of the Highlands; at 16, they may be interested to hear the 'truth about Bonnie Prince Charlie'; at 21 they are doing research on the eighteenth-century Scottish community in Rome. Nelson provides another familiar example of a spiral. For children of 8, he lies romantically wounded on deck (perhaps they can visit the *Victory*); by 12 they may be more interested in the fact that he was commanding highly sophisticated sailing vessels, some of them will be reading the 'Hornblower' stories, and they may have a detailed knowledge of nautical terms; at 16 they will be interested in Lady Hamilton and the moral code of the Hanoverians (you might show them the Olivier film); at 24, they may be doing research on the victualling of naval vessels in the 1790s.

In progressing through such spirals, the child is making use of:

(a) material he encounters in everyday life, in conversation, in books, radio and television, either casually or as the result of interest.

(b) material introduced to him and made available to him when he is actually doing historical projects in the school.

(c) material which he encounters in other projects, for instance in geography, English and religious studies, which gives background to the topic, puts it in perspective, and provides comparisons and analogies.

(d) a deepening of response as a result of 'maturing' or 'growing-up'. In choosing material for a topic at a particular level, and in determining a method of treatment, a teacher should bear in mind not only the previous learning experience of the child, but the probable future course of his experience in this area of understanding.

Topics and other techniques

Much of the argument so far has implied that the normal method of organizing historical work in the school should be by topic, patch, project or, as Wake preferred, probe (1969, p. 153 sq.). The topic approach is indeed consistent with our theoretical position, that the basic unit of history is a historical response, and with Elton and Marwick's views about the importance of 'events' and 'unique events'. It follows from the psychological account of stimulating a series of associations, from the establishment of a chronological scheme out of a series of isolated episodes and from the notion of the progressive refinement of historical stereotypes. The conception of a historical response also fits well with the kinds of techniques we have been discussing. The teacher introduces the children to a topic, sometimes a stereotyped subject, or new material which goes a little beyond known stereotypes. He stimulates a flow of associations in class discussion, then allows the children in group work to bring out associated material more familiar to them, and finally gives them opportunities to pursue their own fantasies and associations in 'research', reading, writing and art (Fairley, 1970, Chapters 3-5). In the course of rounding-off the project with the making of class books, an anthology, a visual display or exhibition, he attempts a discreet analysis of the material, makes some more links, and indicates a structure within the material.

But if the individual exploration of the material is essential in historical learning, this does not mean that the teacher must abdicate. The history teacher has a series of dynamic parts to play. In the first place, enthusiasm, for the history teacher as for any other, is infectious; a keen and able teacher acts as a reference figure for the class—they may want (at least for a day or two) to be keen and able historians themselves (Bruner, 1960, p. 90). Lecturers of course have the same influence on undergraduates. Second, because most historical material can only be encountered at second-hand through various media of communication, the teacher can reasonably see himself as one of the media. It may well be, for instance, in some circumstances appropriate to communicate the story of Charles I's execution by reading, or asking the class to read, a passage by C. V. Wedgwood. But it may also be appropriate with a particular class for the teacher to tell the story in his own words. This can be equally true of the analytical talk. A digest of the views of Hartwell and

Hobsbawm on standards of living in the Industrial Revolution might be an excellent method of introducing the topic. But a teacher may feel that an account of the controversy structured by himself with a group of children in mind will be equally effective. Finally, the rambling, reminiscent associational talk or, where possible, dialogue, has been traditionally effective in stimulating interest and personal reflection among the listeners. As well as the bad history teachers who read out potted notes for us to copy, we all remember those for whom the tactics of Marston Moor were an obsession and who moved boxes of chalk around the front desks in simulation of Napoleon's armies. In secondary schools, history teachers have to make a greater personal contribution than in the middle school. Unless normal secondary children are engaged in really exacting project work with very good materials, they become readily bored with small pieces of research and writing. They are more interested in the teacher as a person, they want to watch him in action, to hear his views, to attract his attention by asking questions and to argue with him. An inspirational talk followed by a vigorous discussion can be a successful technique for history teaching at this level.

The inspirational teacher is an essential part of history teaching—but only a part. He must learn not to go on and on, not to smother his audience's imaginative powers with an indigestible wadge of his own associations. He has to know when to retire from the scene, and when to allow his class the opportunity to respond to the historical material in their own way.

Topics and essays

The project-topics of junior education are conventionally replaced in secondary and higher education by essay-topics or research topics; that is, the basic shape of introductory lesson/discussion/tutorial, followed by work by the students (sometimes individually, sometimes co-operative), then by presentation of the work (in a frieze, model, class book, essay or thesis), completed by discussion or teacher's comment (orally or in writing), remains the same, while the work becomes progressively more analytical. The Oxbridge pattern—introduction of an essay subject, with a suggested list of books and articles; reading and writing by the student amounting perhaps to an average of two working days during the following week, and discussion of the essay at the next tutorial—is essentially similar to the introduction, class activity, tidying-up of the infant school. Similarly, an undergraduate may be asked to write on only eight detailed topics during his coverage of one substantial period, and if he does not attend the (optional) lectures and is contemptuous of outline histories, he may never cover the whole period at all; so that the resulting approach is similar to a topic coverage of history in the school.

The length of time set aside for any one topic will clearly vary with the organization of the timetable, the concentration span of the student, and the depth of treatment required. A workable pattern in the middle school is of four 'double-period' sessions of between $1\frac{1}{2}$ and 2 hours, or a total of 6-8 hours. A normal ten-year-old will almost certainly show signs of flagging interest beyond this time. In higher education, an average student may devote between ten and twenty hours to an essay; if he is given more time, he will probably only leave the essay until three or four days before it is due. In secondary education, where the topic method is less often used and where the treatment is more staccato and chronological, a norm is probably about three hours of classroom work, followed by a homework essay which if diligently done may take another three.

How the given block of time is broken up obviously

depends on the timetable of each institution. But our interpretation of the psychology of learning history suggests that after the presentation of a topic, a period for the realization of immediate associational links is required; in other words, an initial presentation lasting perhaps half-an-hour can be usefully followed by perhaps an hour's reading, writing, art or other activity. There should then be one or more intervals of time in which the less immediate associational material can manifest itself (see C. S. Forester's account of the increasing number of barnacles on his plank), and finally a sustained drive to a deadline, pulling the resultant material into shape. This is in fact how both the middle school pattern of a project, followed by activity leading to display, and the university pattern of essay topic, followed by three or four days' discursive reading, then two or three days of 'getting it done on time', actually work.

Topics and a curriculum

Thus far we have argued for a history curriculum to consist of a series of distinct topics introduced by the teacher and developed by the pupils over several units of study. In that sense, the curriculum is structured and didactic; the topics are not chosen by the pupils themselves. They are chosen by the teacher, head of department or curriculum planning group to provide a series of learning experiences in history which develop a sense of pure history and facilitate applications of history relevant to the children concerned. We should hope that each topic would be chosen to embody one or several of the concepts discussed in Chapters 3 and 4, and with the intention of making a cumulative contribution to the children's experience of the subject. Within the structure, the harnessing of each child's distinctive contribution to the process, and the development of his spontaneous interests, can be provided for by giving a wide choice of follow-up activities, by flexible organization of the classroom during these activities, and by the sympathetic reception of the work produced.

We can now go on to indicate the range and scope of topics for a school history curriculum. We can begin with two basic components—'events' and 'people'. It has already been argued that the short narrative sequence, the event, is the vocabulary of history, and thus it is the basic topic form: the Boston Tea Party, Napoleon's taking of the Imperial crown and the assassination at Sarajevo, are examples of 'events' around which the children's work can be developed. Second, there is the series of linked events which make up the stereotyped form of a 'life'. In spite of Elton's reservations, there is no doubt that biography should be a key component of school history, both as 'The Life of John Smith' and as 'The Life and Times of John Smith'. It is a kind of history which embodies a number of the criteria outlined above—the study of people in time, and of people changing in time, chance, the study of people who died young and of people who were long-lived. A life-span, indeed, provides an admirable unit of the curriculum and framework of a topic; the way in which society changes within the life-span of an individual, the contribution which an individual may make to social change, and the extent to which the individual adapts himself to change, are clearly key historical questions.

At the same time, we can recognize the limitations of the biography and the need to provide some complementary topics. Single biographies are less effective in portraying the notion of generational time, the understanding that at any moment society contains a series of generations each with a different sense of past, present and future. For a fuller historical experience (the dynamic model of Chapter 3), we shall want to study a succession of generations coming to maturity and each embodying its sense of the present in its actions and institutional arrangements. Similarly, a biographical study cannot give us an adequate picture of the transmission of human culture beyond the memory span of individuals; we thus need to examine the culture at a second point when all the individuals alive at a given first point are dead. This suggests a length of years close to the conventional 'century' as an optimum period of study; it will show at least three or four 'generations' at their successive phases of maturity, and the culture transmitted across them. Beyond about a hundred years, children certainly, and many adults, will find it difficult to keep their grasp on the various threads of interest; some surnames of the period, for instance, will begin to disappear, and family connections to become tenuous. We can tolerate, therefore, chronological gaps between the periods chosen for study. Beyond the century, the treatment will have to be more attenuated and thematic (involving of course a danger of over-abstraction). But such surveys, as we have seen, will be useful in suggesting how topics can be linked together into chronological sequences, and in providing the broad sweep which Namier asks for. These survey topics will be a modified form of the lines of development which have sometimes been excessively used in school history teaching (Burston, 1963, p. 136).

This discussion then suggests a typology of four chronological units—the 'event' (e.g., the battle of Hastings, the first Reform Bill), the 'life and times' (William the Conqueror, Lord John Russell), the century (the Norman kings, nineteenth-century England), and the survey topic (church windows from the conquest to the Reformation; parliamentary elections in English novels). The 'event' and the 'life' will occur more frequently in a curriculum for children; the survey is already a familiar device; the century is probably most sophisticated, and may be attempted latest and least often. Simple junior school sequences then might be: Salamis (event), Alfred (life), the Armada (event),

Nelson (life), Ships through the Ages (thematic survey), the Tudors (century); or Thermopylae (event), Julius Caesar (life), Hastings (event), Oliver Cromwell (life), spears, bows and guns (survey), the Stuarts (century). In practice, we might want to mix topics from both sequences (and others) across two or three years of work, in order to make the curriculum spiral rather than linear.

Local history and field-work

Under the leadership of W. G. Hoskins, H. P. R. Finberg, Maurice Beresford and others there has been a very substantial growth of interest in local history in Britain in the past twenty years. But many professional historians have either completely ignored this area of work, or have discussed it as a peripheral activity; and this has had its effect on examination syllabuses and on history curricula in secondary schools. No one, of course, would wish to assert that local history should be the only kind of history, or that other kinds of history should not be taught in schools. What is in question is the rather odd proposition that the only important kind of history is that dealing with the nation-state or larger institutions. It is in fact not true, as Elton asserts, that the workings of the central organs of the state are so crucial to the functioning of society that they should engross the attention of all proper historians. Of course they form a part, an important part, of the framework of historic societies. But until quite recently, the lives of most people for much of the time have been at least as influenced by factors outside the control of the state—social norms, primitive beliefs, soils, weather, harvests, local resources, disease and mortality, population trends—and these topics are often best treated within a local regional or provincial framework, or sometimes across national boundaries (Finberg, 1962).

Within its geographical units, local history has all the

characteristics which have been suggested as distinctive of history—events, people, people changing in time, social groups and so on. And as for the importance of evidence, we can often make much more effective use in the school of evidence from local history, from records offices, museums, field-work, local memory and the like, than we can of collections of selected, edited and translated documents from national history. The major practical disadvantage, that the material at local levels is normally much less well documented and worked over than that at national level (we know less of our Civil War skirmish than we do about Marston Moor), can be an advantage—it forces the teacher to be his own historian, to use the tools of the trade and be seen to be doing so by the pupils (see the introduction to Corfe, 1970).

I have elsewhere distinguished between environmental studies (the integrated study of the local environment) and field-work (work outside the school as part of the study of a traditional subject). Historical field-work can itself be seen to have two functions—to illustrate general historical themes (talk about the Normans and visit a Norman church) or as an integral part of local history (study the development of the local church). We could talk in fact of applied local history and pure local history, and give both a place in the school curriculum.

We should not regard field-work as a special or unusual school activity: it is merely the use of one kind of evidence which is relevant to some historical topics. Field-work has the advantage of being the easiest and cheapest way of enabling children to encounter first-hand historical evidence, evidence which is not a duplicated extract or a photocopied manuscript or a photograph in a book, but is the thing itself, the Jacobean panelling, the milestone or the tan-yard. In the field, junior as well as secondary school children can sometimes do simple pieces of original historical work, using the numbers in a class to advantage;

summarizing the information given on gravestones perhaps, or listing all the dated buildings in a village. And keen-eyed children may pick out details which no one has noticed before. Children surprisingly often find discrepancies and inadequacies both in the secondary texts they are using—on a detail of heraldry, for instance, or armour of a medieval effigy—and in the background information which the teacher has given them: and thus they have an immediate introduction to the controversies and probabilities of history. Field-work presents difficulties of course. It is expensive, not always easy to organize, sometimes hazardous to carry out, and it requires careful preparation and follow-up. In the suggested programmes in Table 2, a limited number of field-work projects have therefore been included in the summer months.

Suggested topics

In making some suggestions for syllabus content, we shall assume a normal middle school which devotes to history a double-period or afternoon each week. If four weeks are given to each topic, and allowing for holidays, sports days, examinations and the like, nine topics might be covered in the school year (in annual programmes of varying intensity, as in Table 1, the peak years might contain eighteen or more topics taken fortnightly).

Following the suggestion made above, we might prepare three syllabuses: one of two years and another of three years, for the first two years of a junior school (7-9) and for three years of a middle school (between 8+ and 13+), the years to be arranged at the headmaster's discretion, and one for the 'nadir' year of the secondary school. The junior school syllabus is based on familiar stories which introduce father-figures and give the children opportunities to identify with people in the past, and which include illness, ageing and death as well as animal stories among the themes. The topics are arranged in a broad chronological sequence, moving first forwards, then backwards.

The middle school syllabus takes a socializing viewpoint, that children should be familiar with some of the principal episodes in British history, but it also begins to introduce Europe and the world, and to move from personal stories to more abstract topics. Imaginative stories are complemented by concrete material and by attention to evidence, and history is brought out of a stereotyped Stone Age into the family and the streets. The topics are again arranged roughly chronologically, moving first forward, then backwards, then forward again in time, to reinforce the notions of chronological sequence and of cause-effect or effect-cause. Events, lives, centuries and survey topics are included, and field-work is done in the summer months. A spiral pattern is incorporated, themes introduced at 7 or 8 (e.g. the Romans) reappearing two or three times in different and more complex forms. Villains as well as heroes, and some human errors, begin to appear, and the opportunity is given for debate.

The topics suggested for a secondary school year continue various themes, while ranging more widely and attempting to provide a stimulating variety in that year. In each case the title is followed by very brief examples of the kind of material that might be utilized. For detailed guidance on methods and materials, see Burston and Green, the *Handbook for History Teachers*, 1962; Carpenter (1964), Ferguson (1967), Fines (1969) and Fairley (1970), and consult your librarian.

Table 2   Topics

Junior school
Age 7+ — 8+

September	The Stone Age (*Stig of the Dump*, Mammoths)
October	Greek Stories (Polyphemus, Daedalus)

November	Roman Stories (geese on the Capitol, Hannibal's elephants)
January	Alfred the Great (young Alfred, Danes, cakes and ships)
February	William the Conqueror (Bayeux tapestry frieze)
March	Richard the Lionheart (Crusaders, Robin Hood, death)
May	Pirates, highwaymen and smugglers (*Treasure Island*, Dick Turpin)
June	Nelson (young Nelson, ships, death)
July	Visit to the local museum (make a class museum)

Age 8+ — 9+

September	Railways (visit a station, George Stephenson)
October	Cook, Clive and Wolfe (Pacific Ocean, India, Canada)
November	Bonnie Prince Charlie (Scotland, escape, songs)
January	Elizabeth (young Elizabeth, dress, buildings)
February	Henry V (young Henry, Kate, Agincourt)
March	Julius Caesar and the Romans (the Ancient Britons, Boudicca)
May	Visit a Roman site (make a model)
June	Alexander the Great (Near East and India)
July	Canals (visit, model, frieze)

Middle school

Age 9+ or 10+

September	Stonehenge (visit it or similar site, model)
October	Imperial Rome (chariots, gladiators, slaves, galleys)
November	Richard III (Wars of the Roses, Princes in the Tower)
January	The Armada (Drake, South and Central America)
February	Puritans and Cavaliers (*Children of the New Forest*)
March	Waterloo (Napoleon, Wellington, military tactics)
May	Water-mills (visit, photographs, model)
June	Second World War (Hitler, Churchill, Battle of Britain)

July — Nineteenth-century buildings (field-work, photographs, frieze)

Age 10+ or 11+

September	First World War (songs, aeroplanes and tanks, Lawrence of Arabia)
October	Queen Victoria (young Victoria, stamps and coins, ageing)
November	The American Colonies (*The Last of the Mohicans*, Boston Tea Party)
January	Charles I (his youth, his queen, execution)
February	Elizabethan dress (Shakespeare, London, Globe Theatre)
March	Henry VIII (his youth, his wives, monasteries)
May	The medieval wool-trade (*The Woolpack*, spinning and weaving)
June	Churches (visit and record three local churches)
July	Visit Iron-Age site (plan, model)

Age 11+ or 12+

September	*The Odyssey* (feature-film, Mediterranean, the suitors)
October	The Black Death (*Piers Plowman*, Chaucer medical detail)
November	Mary Queen of Scots (Scotland, Elizabeth, death)
January	Dickens's London (feature-film, the novels, Mayhew)
February	American Civil War (feature-film, songs, Lincoln)
March	Schools from 1870 to today (field-work, log-books, models)
May	Roads (local survey, old maps, milestones)
June	Gordon and Omdurman (Churchill's early life)
July	Monasteries (visits, plans, model, documents)

Secondary school

Autumn term	USA—Lincoln to Vietnam (music, *Citizen Kane*)
	Crete: the Minotaur, Minos, archaeology, Second World War (colour film, Waugh's *Officers and Gentlemen*)
Spring term	The Boer War and South Africa (colour film, Imperialism, race and colour)

	Victorian morality (Mayhew to Longford, use Chaplin's *Easy Street*)
Summer term	Blacksmiths (local survey, tools and techniques, make a film)
	The Aztecs, the Spaniards, and modern Mexico (colour film, cruelty and race, student unrest)

Conclusion

This book began by drawing attention to a paradox; the contrast between the 'doubt and discontent' among history teachers and the great vitality shown by the kinds of history that most of their pupils are experiencing (Chapter 1). A number of causes of doubt were identified and two were chosen for extended treatment: the philosophical doubt about whether 'history' as defined by professional historians is something meaningful to children and ordinary people, and the psychological doubt about whether children are capable of making valid responses to historical material. We could summarize our answer to these doubts rather brutally by saying that if these theories require us to dismiss what a great many people have been enjoyably doing for the past two hundred years under the name of history, then there must be something wrong with the theories and not the people. And when a grave researcher tells us that children do not possess conceptual equipment vital to historical understanding until middle adolescence, we shall be inclined to refute him in the manner of Samuel Johnson with the stone. We shall turn to the nearest eight-year-old and ask him to tell us something about the *Ivanhoe* series currently running on television.

Chapters 2 and 3 were intended to give reasoned support to this intuitive reaction. Chapter 3 attacked the philosophical problem by extracting from such distinguished sources as Dewey, Collingwood, and Trevor-Roper a view of history in which the reader or *consumer* is given the central role, and in which history is seen as 'existing' whenever someone responds to a true past event. So that as soon as we find a child who really believes that once upon a time Britons stood shoulder to shoulder in squares on a battlefield called Waterloo, then we are indeed 'doing' history in the primary school. As to how a child 'thinks' about history, Chapter 2 was inclined to agree that he might not think very logically or even rationally about it, but he could think imaginatively, intuitively, and in concrete detail, and that it was most important that he should do so, because he ought to be developing these capacities for employment in adult life. The proposition that children were capable of responding to 'pure' history having been accepted, Chapter 4 went on to the ways in which historical material can be applied to other purposes in the school, in particular, as a form of vicarious experience contributing to the emotional and social development of the child. Finally, Chapter 5 attempted to show that the conclusions from the theoretical arguments in the previous chapters could indeed be embodied in practical arrangements for teaching in the school.

In the past ten years or so, we have seen in history teaching the Emperor's new clothes situation in reverse. Too many of us have been persuaded that Clio had no clothes. In fact, if we just rub our eyes, we shall find that she has always been richly and colourfully dressed : and the children have known it all the time.

Further reading

Chapter 1

BARRACLOUGH, G. (1967), *History and the Common Man*. Barraclough's bold plea, in an address to the Historical Association, to stop 'mulling over Simon de Montfort for ever'.

CARR, E. H. (1961), *What is History?* A pleasantly written book, putting a now unfashionable case for 'History as Progress'.

FORESTER, C. S. (1967), *Long before Forty*. Forester's autobiography. A fascinating glimpse of a child engaged in one kind of learning, and of the gestation of one kind of historical writing.

SELLAR, W. C. and YEATMAN, R. J. (1960), *1066 and All That*, Penguin Books. Essential reading for the serious student.

TREVOR-ROPER, H. R. (1957), *History: Professional and Lay*. Trevor-Roper's inaugural address, in which he pithily put the case that 'the humane subjects ... exist primarily not for the training of professionals but for the education of laymen'.

Chapter 2

BALLARD, M., ed. (1970), *New Movements in the Study and Teaching of History*, Temple Smith. Contains some useful articles, including Hallam's over-pessimistic review of 'Piaget and Thinking in History', and Elton having second thoughts on school history teaching.

BURSTON, W. H. and THOMPSON, D., eds (1967), *Studies in the Nature and Teaching of History*. Together with some over-theoretical articles, the volume includes Peel's interpretation of research on aspects of the learning of history.

COLTHAM, J. B. (1971), *The Development of Thinking and The Learning of History*, Historical Association. An interesting Piagetian approach to the topic.

MCKELLAR, P. (1968), *Experience and Behaviour*. A wide-ranging survey of many aspects of psychology, particularly suggestive on the part played by irrational processes in thinking.

SUTHERLAND, M. (1971), *Everyday Imagining and Education*. Much-needed review of the nature of imagination and its role in education. Chapters 7 and 8 are particularly relevant to our purpose.

VYGOTSKY, L. S. (1962), *Thought and Language*. A perceptive and blessedly short book by a Russian psychologist, which has helped to re-establish the role of the teacher in the classroom.

Chapter 3

BURSTON, W. H. (1963), *Principles of History Teaching*. Burston attempts in his dry-as-dust manner to span the gap between theory and the classroom.

COLLINGWOOD, R. G. (1946), *The Idea of History*. Necessary though dated reading for the advanced student; indigestible for the beginner. Nowadays more interesting as a picture of Collingwood than as an account of History.

COLTHAM, J. B. and FINES, J. (1971), *Educational Objectives and the Study of History*, Historical Association. A systematic Bloomian approach to historical objectives.

ELTON, G. R. (1967), *The Practice of History*. A short, pugnacious book by a straight-line professional, as Marwick would call him. Worth reading and indeed widely read, but not to be taken too seriously by those interested in school history teaching.

MARWICK, A. (1970), *The Nature of History*. Don't be put off by Marwick's prose style. Plough on, and you will find that he covers a great deal of ground and says many pertinent things.

STERN, F., ed (1956), *Varieties of History*, Meridian. A very useful collection of extracts, some of them not easily available in their original format.

Chapter 4

FAIRLEY, J. A. (1970), *Patch History and Creativity*. Starting from a point of view similar to that taken in Chapter 2, Fairley elaborates an account of practical techniques and syllabus content.

FINES, J., ed. (1969), *History*. Fines's lively introduction, which touches on vicarious experience and other themes of the present volume, is followed by useful chapters on the materials for particular periods.

GESELL, A., ILG, F. L. and AMES, L. D. (1956), *Youth: The Years from Ten to Sixteen*. Gesell's now ageing survey is still the best starting-point for thinking about the needs of children at a particular age.

PLOWDEN REPORT (1967), *Children and their Primary Schools*, Vol. 1. Plowden's section on history is one of the more perceptive in that massive pot-pourri.

SCHOOLS COUNCIL (1968), *Young School Leavers*. A very interesting account of the attitudes of children, parents and teachers to the education of fifteen-year-olds.

Chapter 5

BURSTON, W. H. and GREEN, C. W. (1962), *Handbook for History Teachers*, Methuen. Introductory articles by Burston, Davies, Perry and others, followed by detailed lists of books and visual aids.

CARPENTER, P. C. (1964), *History Teaching: The Era Approach*. A brief clear argument for a non-chronological approach to history teaching.

CORFE, T., ed. (1970), *History in the Field*. An excellent practical introduction to historical field-work.

DOUCH, R. (1967), *Local History and the Teacher*, Routledge & Kegan Paul. Interesting introduction by Douch, followed by sections on 'Sources of Local History' and 'Local History Studies in School and College'.

SCHOOLS COUNCIL (1969), *Humanities for the Young School Leaver: An Approach through History*. A lively booklet which yet shows some signs of having been written by a committee.

Students should also refer to the volumes of *Teaching History* (Historical Association), 1969—. The many useful articles include Murphy, Steel and Taylor on family history, Vodden and Blench on museums, Barlow and Isenberg on drama, Happer and Blyth on model-making, Cook on local history, Salt on field-work and Fines on recent research.

Bibliography

ANTHONY, S. (1940), *The Child's Discovery of Death*, Routledge & Kegan Paul.

BARRACLOUGH, G. (1966), *History and the Common Man*, Historical Association.

BARRACLOUGH, G. (1967), *An Introduction to Contemporary History*, Penguin Books.

BLOCH, M. (1954), *The Historian's Craft*, Manchester U.P.

BLOOM, B. S. *et al.* (1956), *Taxonomy of Educational Objectives*, Vol. 1, Longmans.

BOOTH, M. B. (1969), *History Betrayed?*, Longmans.

BOYLE, D. G. (1969), *A Student's Guide to Piaget*, Pergamon.

BRUNER, J. S., GOODNOW, J. J. and AUSTIN, G. A. (1956), *A Study of Thinking*, New York: Wiley.

BRUNER, J. S. (1960), *The Process of Education*, New York: Vintage Books.

BRUNER, J. S. (1966), *Toward a Theory of Instruction*, Belknap Harvard.

BURSTON, W. H. (1963), *Principles of History Teaching*, Methuen.

BURSTON, W. H. and THOMPSON, D., eds (1967), *Studies in Nature and Teaching of History*, Routledge & Kegan Paul.

BIBLIOGRAPHY

CARPENTER, P. C. (1964), *History Teaching: The Era Approach*, Cambridge U.P.

CARR, E. H. (1961), *What is History?*, Macmillan.

CENTRAL ADVISORY COUNCIL FOR EDUCATION (England) (1959), *15 to 18* (Crowther Report, vol. 1), HMSO.

CENTRAL ADVISORY COUNCIL FOR EDUCATION (England) (1963), *Half our Future* (Newsom Report), HMSO.

CENTRAL ADVISORY COUNCIL FOR EDUCATION (England) (1967), *Children and their Primary Schools* (Plowden Report), HMSO.

COLLINGWOOD, R. G. (1946), *The Idea of History*, Oxford U.P.

CORFE, T., *ed.* (1970), *History in the Field*, Blond.

CROWTHER REPORT, *see* Central Advisory Council for Education.

DEWEY, J. (1916), *Democracy and Education*, Macmillan.

ELTON, G. R. (1967), *The Practice of History*, Fontana.

ELTON, G. R. (1970), 'What Sort of History Should we Teach?', in *New Movements in the Study and Teaching of History*, ed. M. Ballard, Temple Smith.

FAIRLEY, J. S. (1970), *Patch History and Creativity*, Longmans.

FERGUSON, S. (1967), *Projects in History*, Batsford.

FINBERG, H. P. R. (1962), 'Local History', in *Approaches to History*, ed. Finberg, Routledge & Kegan Paul.

FINES, J. (1968), 'Archives in Schools', in *History*, liii, p. 348.

FINES, J., ed. (1969), *History*, Blond.

FORESTER, C. S. (1967), *Long Before Forty*, Michael Joseph.

GABRIEL, J. (1968), *Children Growing Up*, Unibooks.

GAGNÉ, R. M. (1965), *The Conditions of Learning*, New York: Holt, Rinehart & Winston.

GESELL, A., ILG, F. L. and AMES, L. B. (1956), *Youth: The Years from Ten to Sixteen*, New York: Harper.

GOMEZ, S. (1968), 'Teaching History on the Elementary School Level', in *The Teaching of History*, ed. J. S. Pocock, Peter Owen.

HALLAM, R. N. (1967), 'Logical Thinking in History', in *Educational Review*, xix, June.

HEBB, D. O. (1949), *The Organization of Behaviour*, New York: Wiley.

HUDSON, L. (1966), *Contrary Imaginations*, Penguin Books.

HUIZINGA, J. (1956), 'Historical Conceptualization', in *The Varieties of History*, ed. F. Stern, Meridian.

ISAACS, N. (1961), *The Growth of Understanding in the Young Child*, Ward Lock.

JAMES, W. (1904), *Psychology*, Macmillan.

JENKINS, R. (1964), *Asquith*, Collins.

JONES, G. E. (1970a), 'Towards a Theory of History Teaching', in *History*, lv, p. 54.

JONES, R. B. (1970b), 'Towards a New History Syllabus', in *History*, lv, p. 384.

KRATHWOHL, D. A. *et al.* (1964), *Taxonomy of Educational Objectives*, vol. 2, Longmans.

MCKELLAR, P. (1957), *Imagination and Thinking*, Cohen & West.

MCKELLAR, P. (1968), *Experience and Behaviour*, Penguin Books.

MARWICK, A. (1970), *The Nature of History*, Macmillan.

MARWICK, A. *et al.* (1971), *What History is and Why it is Important*, Open University.

NAMIER, L. (1956), 'History and Political Culture', in *The Varieties of History*, ed. F. Stern, Meridian.

NEWSOM REPORT, *see* Central Advisory Council for Education.

PARES, R. (1961), *The Historian's Business*, Oxford U.P.

PEEL, E. A. (1960), *The Pupil's Thinking*, Oldbourne.

PEEL, E. A. (1967), 'Some Problems in the Psychology of History Teaching', in *Studies in the Nature and Teaching of History*, ed. W. H. Burston and D. Thompson, Routledge & Kegan Paul.

PIAGET, J. (1926), *The Language and Thought of the Child*, Routledge & Kegan Paul, 1932 edition.

BIBLIOGRAPHY

PIAGET, J. (1928), *Judgment and Reasoning in the Child*, Routledge & Kegan Paul.

PLOWDEN REPORT, *see* Central Advisory Council for Education.

PLUMB, J. H. (1964), *A Crisis in the Humanities*, Penguin Books.

PRICE, H. H. (1953), *Thinking and Experience*, Hutchinson.

PRICE, M. (1968), 'History in Danger', in *History*, liii, no. 179 (October), p. 342.

REEVES, J. W. (1965), *Thinking about Thinking*, Secker & Warburg.

RYLE, G. (1949), *The Concept of Mind*, Hutchinson.

SCHOOLS COUNCIL (1968), *Young School Leavers*.

SCHOOLS COUNCIL (1969), *Humanities for the Young School Leaver; An Approach through History*.

SCHOOLS COUNCIL/NUFFIELD (1970), *The Humanities Project: an Introduction*, Heinemann.

SHERIF, M. and SHERIF, C. W. (1956), *An Outline of Social Psychology*, Harper & Row.

SHERIF, M. and SHERIF, C. W. (1969), *Social Psychology*, Harper International.

STEEL, D. and TAYLOR, L. (1969), 'History Through the Family: II', in *Teaching History*, ll, p. 9.

STEEL, D. and TAYLOR, L. (1971), *Family History in Schools*, Phillimore, Chichester.

SULLIVAN, E. V. (1967), *Piaget and the School Curriculum: A Critical Appraisal*, The Ontario Institute for Studies in Education, Bulletin 2.

SUTHERLAND, M. B. (1971), *Everyday Imagining and Education*, Routledge & Kegan Paul.

THOMPSON, E. P. (1963), *The Making of the English Working Class*, Gollancz.

THOMSON, G. H. (1924), *Instinct, Intelligence and Character*, Allen & Unwin.

TREVOR-ROPER, H. R. (1957), *History: Professional and Lay*, Oxford U.P.

TREVOR-ROPER, H. R. (1971), 'Sir Walter Scott and History', in *Listener*, 86, No. 2212.

VYGOTSKY, L. S. (1962), *Thought and Language*, M.I.T. Press.

WAKE, R. (1969), 'History as a Separate Discipline', in *Teaching History*, 1, p. 243.

WALL, W. D. (1948), *The Adolescent Child*, Methuen.

WATTS, D. G. (1969), *Environmental Studies*, Routledge & Kegan Paul.

WATTS, D. G., (1971), 'Environmental Studies, Perception and Judgment', in *General Education*, no. 16 (spring), pp. 20-5.

WISEMAN, S., ed. (1967), *Intelligence and Ability*, Penguin Books.